Middle School

Nonfiction Comprehension

Reading Strategies for the Content Areas

Students learn much about their world through reading. Fiction, through illustration, tells them about people and human nature. Nonfiction, through information, tells them what the world is like. Just as certain skills are needed to gain a deeper understanding of fiction, so are certain skills needed to gain the most from nonfiction. The purpose of this book is to help teachers to pass on those nonfiction skills to young readers so they can move from learning to read to reading to learn.

As students progress through the grades, their reading load increases and changes. Students may encounter an increased volume of text. They may have to deal with new vocabulary and new concepts in each content area. They may lack prior knowledge to apply to new information. They may have a basic unfamiliarity with expository text features. They may be asked to show their understanding of nonfiction selections on standardized tests. This book includes reading selections and techniques to help teachers to overcome these common hurdles that students face.

This book is especially appropriate for:

- Reading teachers who want to provide extra nonfiction practice using specific comprehension skills;
- Teachers in other disciplines who want to reinforce content-specific comprehension skills;
- Parents who want to provide extra nonfiction reading practice for their child.

A good reader is a good learner. The goal of this book is to make all students good readers!

Use and Organization

Research suggests that "explicit teaching techniques are particularly effective for comprehension strategy instruction. In explicit instruction, teachers tell readers why and when they should use strategies, what strategies they should use, and how to apply them. The steps of explicit instruction typically include direct explanation, teacher modeling ("thinking aloud"), guided practice, and application." (*Put Reading First*, p. 53)

This book includes two types of teacher information pages. The book is divided into six units that identify major comprehension areas. These units are further divided into 16 specific comprehension skills. At the beginning of each unit is a teacher information page that identifies the comprehension skills in that unit and provides background details and recognition strategies for each skill. Each comprehension skill is then covered in a lesson that includes reading selections from a variety of content areas. At the beginning of each lesson is another teaching information page that covers the reading selections in the lesson. Summaries of each selection are provided, along with vocabulary words and writing exercises. Included on this page are approaches to tap prior knowledge, emphasize and reinforce the comprehension skill, preview text features, and help students to comprehend the selection.

Each lesson contains one to three reading selections that emphasize a specific comprehension skill, such as summary or comparison-contrast. Many of the reading selections also contain visual aids that the student can use to gain extra information about the topic. A unit on visual aids prepares the student for the use of these tools. Each reading selection also includes activities that center on comprehension and vocabulary. At the back of the book are a complete answer key and a variety of graphic organizers.

TECHNIQUES to Improve Comprehension

This book offers a variety of comprehension techniques on the teacher information pages. Here are more comprehension techniques that can be used to increase student comprehension.

- Introduce the reading skills of skimming and scanning. Skimming notes the general subject and major headings. Scanning looks for key words.
- Model a fluent reading process: read; stop and think; reread when comprehension breaks down.
- Ask questions that help relate the reading selection to the reader's experiences, emotions, or knowledge.
- Use comparison-contrast to help the students to connect new information to known information.
- Model and require students to create questions about their reading.
- Use graphic organizers to organize and display group thinking, questioning, and learning.
- Help the students to draw conclusions from information the author has provided. Help the students to question their way through the selection.
- Have the students summarize the main points of each selection or section of the reading.
- Provide ways for the students to record changes in their thinking as new information is gathered.

Bibliography

Armbruster, B. B., F. Lehr, and J. Osbourne. *Put Reading First: The Research Building Blocks for Teaching Children to Read.* Washington, D. C.: National Institute for Literacy, 2001.

Skill	Mathematics	Biography	History	Economics	Geography	Earth Science	Life Science	Physical Science	Daily Skills
Diagrams				77		90	7, 9	75	
Graphs	12, 13			12	12, 13	13			
Charts and Time Lines	15, 16, 17		18	17	15	15	89		16, 17
Maps			20, 62, 113		20, 22, 62, 92, 99	22, 92	21		
Main Idea		25, 29	25, 26, 27, 29		29				27, 29
Details					36	36, 37	35		38
Summary			43		40, 41	40			
Narration of Event		47, 49, 51	47, 48, 49, 51		51				48
Narration of Process	55				56	55, 56, 57			
Cause and Effect		60	60, 62, 63		61, 62	62	7		61
Description							71, 72		
Division				77				75	77
Classification				85		82	83		
Comparison-Contrast			91		92	90, 92	89		
Drawing Conclusions		97	95, 96	95, 99	96, 99		96		
Fact or Opinion?			105, 106		105, 107	107			
Purpose and Structure			110, 111, 113		110, 113	109			109

UNIT 1 Visual Aids

We all know the old saying, "A picture is worth a thousand words." The saying is true for visual aids, which includes graphic organizers. These graphic sources range from simple illustrations to complicated graphs and charts. Often, graphic sources such as diagrams, graphs, charts, and maps are skipped over by young readers because they look hard to understand. These visual aids are not hard to understand if students take the time to study them. These graphic sources can give more information in a smaller space than the written word.

Diagrams (Lesson 1)

A diagram is an illustration that is meant to explain rather than represent. It does not try to show the reader what the thing looks like. Instead, it breaks the topic into its parts and arrangement. For example, a diagram of a food chain would show all the members of the chain. It would use arrows to show the arrangement or relationship between the members. Diagrams are very helpful in explaining mathematical or scientific topics.

To understand a diagram:

- Read the title of the diagram or article carefully. What is it about?
- Read all of the labels. Take time to figure out what they mean.
- If the diagram has a caption, read the caption carefully.
- If arrows are used in the diagram, study the movement suggested by the arrows.
- Try to identify all the parts and their relationship to one another.

Graphs (Lesson 2)

A graph is a diagram that uses pictures, points, lines, bars, or areas to show and compare information. A pictograph uses pictures to show information. A bar graph uses bars, and a line graph uses one or more lines to give information. A pie graph uses slices of a round graph to show facts. Some graphs will have two lines or two bars to compare and contrast information. Sometimes students are asked to compare and contrast two graphs.

To understand a graph:

- First, identify the kind of graph.
- Read the title of the graph carefully. What information does the graph show?
- Read the labels on the side and bottom of the graph. Take time to figure out what they mean.
- Follow the bars or lines with your finger.
- Move a finger from the labels to the point on the line or bar to get the information you need.

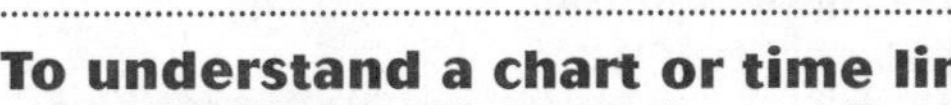

Charts and Time Lines (Lesson 3)

A chart is used to present exact information in an orderly way. Tell the students they use charts every day, such as menus, bus schedules, and TV schedules. Charts arrange facts in a way that makes them easy to read and understand. Often, charts include times or numbers. A flowchart helps to show the order of events in an action. A time line shows the order of events along a vertical or horizontal line.

To understand a chart or time line:

- Read the title of the chart or time line carefully.
- Read all the labels in the chart or time line. Decide what the labels mean.
- Read the times or numbers in the chart or time line.
- Use your finger to follow the rows or columns of a chart, or the movement of the flowchart or time line.
- Be sure you know what information you need and what information the chart or time line gives.

Maps (Lesson 4)

Maps are used to give information about a place. Maps are like a drawing of a place from above. Maps can tell about the boundaries of places. They can tell about the landscape, the climate, or the population. Most maps have the same features, such as a compass rose, a legend or key, and a distance scale.

To understand a map:

- Read the title of the map. What information does the map give?
- Find the compass rose. Run your finger along the points of the rose. Usually, north is toward the top of the map.
- Find the distance scale. Practice measuring a distance on the map.
- Find the legend or key. Look at all the symbols. Take time to figure out what they mean.
- Find some of the symbols on the map.
- Study the map to find the information you need.

Research Base

"Learning how to read informational texts involves strategies such as gathering information, summarizing and synthesizing information, and making connections to prior knowledge. Readers of informational texts must analyze where information is located within the overall organizational framework." (*Guiding Readers and Writers: Grades 3–6*, p. 400)

Diagrams

SELECTION DETAILS

Summary
"Diseases Caused by Viruses" (page 7): This article uses a diagram to show how viruses attack and reproduce in a body cell.
"What Are Trophic Levels?" (page 9): This article uses a diagram to illustrate the trophic levels in a forest food web.

Selection Type
Science Articles

Comprehension Skill
Use Visual Aids for Information

Standards

Reading
- Identify main idea and details.
- Use a variety of appropriate reference materials, including representations of information such as diagrams, maps, and charts, to gather information.

Science
- Recognize the cause and spread of communicable and noncommunicable diseases.
- Categorize organisms according to their roles in food chains and webs.

VOCABULARY

Introduce the vocabulary words. Write the words on the board. Help students find a definition for each word. Have students use each word in a sentence.

"Diseases Caused by Viruses"
viruses *infected*
particles

"What Are Trophic Levels?"
trophic levels *scavengers*

Tap Prior Knowledge

"Diseases Caused by Viruses": Ask the students if they have ever had a cold or chicken pox. How do they think they got that disease?

"What Are Trophic Levels?": Ask the students if they have ever seen a bird eat an insect. If so, they have seen a food web in action. On which level of the food web do the students think they belong?

Skill to Emphasize

Review the section about diagrams on page 5.

Preview Text Features

Point out the diagrams in the articles. Point out the labels and captions in the diagrams about virus reproduction. Point out the labels in the food web diagram. The labels give valuable information about the diagram. Point out the pyramidical shape of the food web; it suggests the trophic levels. Boldfaced words indicate vocabulary words.

Comprehending the Selection

You may wish to model how to identify the main idea in each selection by asking: *What is this article mostly about?* Ask the students how the diagrams help them to learn more about the topic.

Reinforce the Comprehension Skill

Remind the students that a diagram is an illustration that is meant to explain. It breaks the topic into its parts and arrangement. Ask the students how the diagrams in each selection show the parts and arrangement of the parts.

Assess

Have the students complete the activities for each selection.

Have the students draw a diagram that helps to explain a topic they have studied recently in science.

Name ______________________________ Date ____________

Diseases Caused by Viruses

Almost everyone has had a cold or the flu. These diseases are caused by **viruses**. Viruses are not cells. They are very tiny **particles**. Some viruses are a hundred times smaller than bacteria.

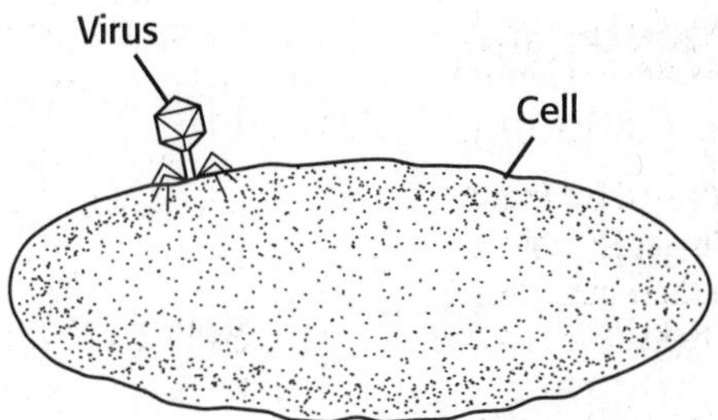

1. A virus enters a cell.

There are many kinds of viruses. All of them cause disease. A virus causes a disease by getting inside a body cell. The virus takes over the cell. It changes the way the cell works. It uses the cell's food. The virus can reproduce inside the cell. Many virus particles are made. Soon the cell bursts open, and all the virus particles pour out. Then they take over other healthy cells.

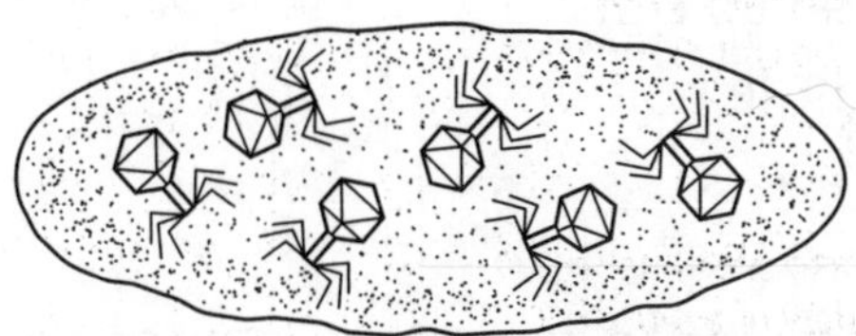

2. A virus reproduces inside the cell.

Besides colds and the flu, viruses can cause other diseases. Measles, chicken pox, and mumps are three other diseases caused by viruses.

Diseases caused by viruses can be spread from one person to another. When a person with a cold or the flu coughs or sneezes, virus particles go into the air. People can breathe the air carrying the virus particles. Then they can get sick, too. Measles and chicken pox can also be spread in this way. You can also get measles by using the towels, dishes, or other objects used by an **infected** person. Chicken pox can be spread in this way, too.

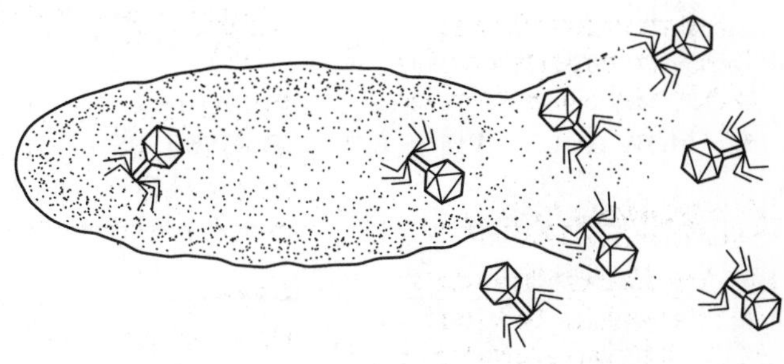

3. Many virus particles burst out of the cell.

Name ______________________________ Date ______________

Comprehension and Vocabulary Review

Darken the circle by the best answer.

1. Colds and flu are caused by _____.
   Ⓐ bacteria
   Ⓑ snow
   Ⓒ viruses
   Ⓓ airplanes

2. Viruses are _____.
   Ⓐ bacteria
   Ⓑ tiny particles
   Ⓒ small cells
   Ⓓ little bombs

3. Viruses reproduce inside _____.
   Ⓐ body cells
   Ⓑ cell phones
   Ⓒ balloons
   Ⓓ explosions

4. *Infected* means _____.
   Ⓐ inside a cell
   Ⓑ entered a fence
   Ⓒ not washed
   Ⓓ has a disease

Write complete sentences to answer each question.

5. What are three diseases caused by viruses?

____

____

6. How does a virus cause a disease?

____

____

7. How does a virus spread from one body cell to another?

____

____

8. What is one way that measles can be spread from one person to another?

____

____

Name ______________________________ Date ______________

What Are Trophic Levels?

Living things that share the same kinds of food are placed in feeding levels, or **trophic levels**. Trophic levels can be arranged from levels that hold the most living things to the levels that hold the fewest living things. The first and largest trophic level is made of producers. This level supports all of the trophic levels above it. Suppose that a food chain is made from an acorn, a rabbit, and a hawk. The oak tree that makes the acorn is a producer. It belongs in the first trophic level. The rabbit that eats the acorn belongs to the next smaller trophic level. And the hawk that eats the rabbit belongs in the last and smallest trophic level.

Why does each trophic level become smaller? Each level shows the movement of the Sun's energy. Producers at the first trophic level change the Sun's energy into food energy. Some of that energy is lost at each trophic level. That means that there are fewer animals in the higher trophic levels because they need more food to stay alive. Most food webs can support only a few trophic levels, with fewer animals in each level.

Some of the energy lost at every trophic level is captured again by **scavengers** and decomposers. Scavengers are animals such as vultures that eat dead animals. Bacteria and fungi, the decomposers, break down dead plants and animals to release the energy stored in their remains. This energy is used by producers.

Humans are part of food webs. They are also part of trophic levels. When they eat plants, humans belong to the second trophic level. They get more energy from their food at this level than at higher levels.

Trophic Levels in a Forest Food Web

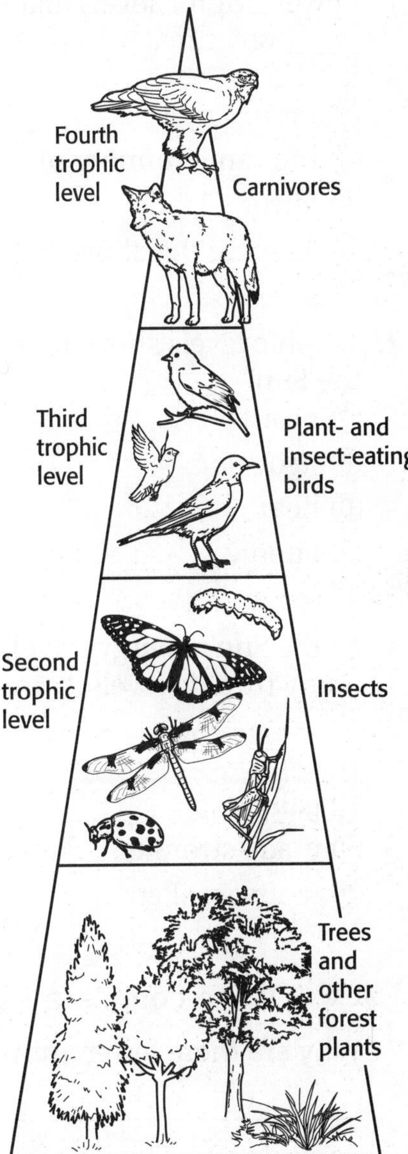

Name ________________________________ Date ______________

Comprehension and Vocabulary Review

Darken the circle by the best answer.

1. Lower trophic levels in a food web have _____ creatures than higher trophic levels.
   Ⓐ more
   Ⓑ the same number of
   Ⓒ fewer
   Ⓓ None of the above

2. Trophic levels show the movement of the Sun's _____.
   Ⓐ orbit
   Ⓑ light
   Ⓒ heat
   Ⓓ energy

3. As the Sun's energy travels through many trophic levels, some of the energy is _____.
   Ⓐ lost
   Ⓑ gained
   Ⓒ made stronger
   Ⓓ made weaker

4. Decomposers _____ food energy at every trophic level.
   Ⓐ destroy
   Ⓑ capture
   Ⓒ lose
   Ⓓ None of the above

5. People get more food energy by eating foods from _____ trophic levels.
   Ⓐ lower
   Ⓑ higher
   Ⓒ the highest
   Ⓓ None of the above

6. _____ are animals that eat dead animals.
   Ⓐ Producers
   Ⓑ Trophics
   Ⓒ Scavengers
   Ⓓ None of the above

Write complete sentences to answer each question.

7. Why are there fewer animals in the higher trophic levels?

____

____

8. If a food web had more than four or five trophic levels, what might happen to the creatures at the highest levels?

____

____

____

____

____

Graphs

Tap Prior Knowledge

"Comparing Line Graphs": Ask the students why the price of gas goes up and down. What economic factors determine how much oil is produced in this country?

"Reading a Climograph": Reinforce the difference between short-term weather events and long-term climate conditions. Ask the students which weather events might be used to determine the climate of an area.

Skill to Emphasize

Review the section about graphs on page 5. Point out the graphs in the selections.

Preview Text Features

Point out the two line graphs in "Comparing Line Graphs." Point out that the scales on the sides and bottoms of the two graphs are different, so the graphs do not give an exact representational comparison. The students must note the points in each graph and how the points correspond to the scales. In "Reading a Climograph," point out that the climograph is really a line graph and a bar graph in one. The label and scale for the line graph are on the left side of the graph, and the label and scale for the bar graph are on the right side of the graph. Abbreviations of the months are on the bottom of the graph.

Comprehending the Selection

Ask the students: *What does each graph show?* Ask the students how the graphs help them to learn more about the topic.

Reinforce the Comprehension Skill

Remind the students that a graph can use pictures, lines, bars, or slices of a circle to show and compare information. Ask the students if they think graphs are a good way to show information.

Assess

Have the students complete the activities for each selection.

Have the students come up with a list of five daily activities. Have them record the length of time they spend on each activity daily. Have the students draw a bar graph that includes 30-minute intervals as the scale.

Have the students search through the newspaper or news magazines for graphs. Bring these graphs to school to share with the class.

SELECTION DETAILS

Summary

"Comparing Line Graphs" (page 12): This article uses two line graphs to compare the production and usage of oil in the United States from 1960 to 1990.

"Reading a Climograph" (page 13): This article uses a climograph to give climate information about Cheyenne, Wyoming.

Selection Type
Social Studies Articles

Comprehension Skill
Use Visual Aids for Information

Standards

Reading
- Use a variety of appropriate reference materials, including representations of information such as diagrams, maps, and charts, to gather information.

Social Studies
- Investigate trends in the consumption and production of renewable and nonrenewable resources.
- Describe large-scale and local weather systems.

Name ______________________________ Date ______________

Comparing Line Graphs

The line graphs below show how much oil was produced and how much was used in the United States per day from 1960 to 1990.

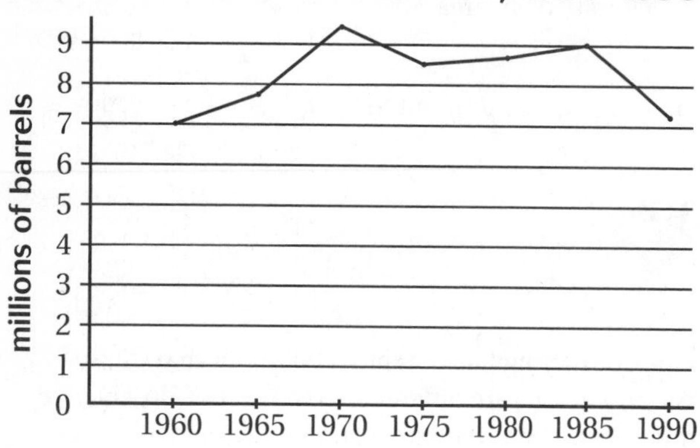

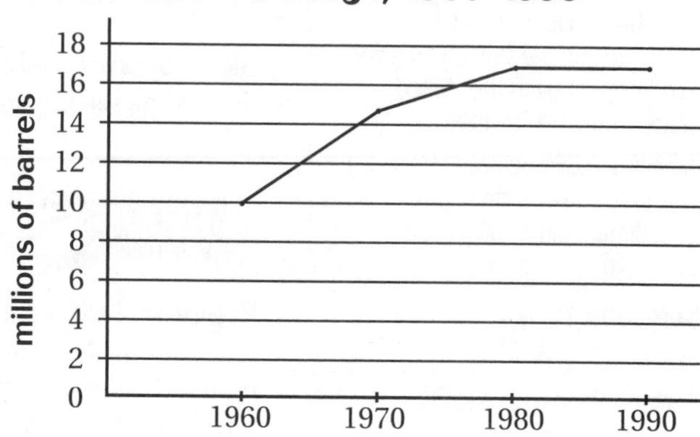

Study the graphs. Then write complete sentences to answer the questions.

1. About how many millions of barrels of oil did the United States produce per day in 1960? ______________________________

2. About how many millions of barrels of oil did the United States produce per day in 1990? ______________________________

3. How did the United States oil production change between 1960 and 1990?

   ____

4. About how many millions of barrels of oil did the United States use per day in 1960?

   ____

5. About how many millions of barrels of oil did the United States use per day in 1990?

   ____

6. What was the trend in United States oil usage between 1960 and 1990?

   ____

7. Look at your answers to questions 3 and 6. Were the United States oil production and oil usage in balance? What conclusion can you draw?

   ____

   ____

   ____

   ____

Name ________________________ Date ______________

Reading a Climograph

The climograph below combines a bar graph and a line graph to give climate information about Cheyenne, Wyoming. Study the graph carefully to see what kind of information is presented.

Use the graph to answer the questions. Darken the circle by the best answer.

Climograph for Cheyenne, Wyoming

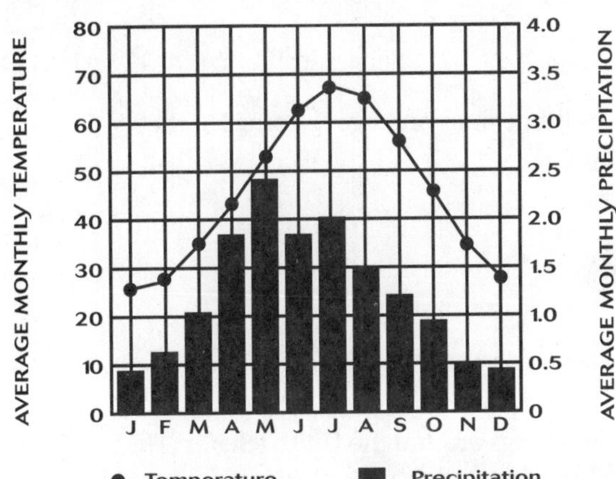

1. During which month does Cheyenne receive the most precipitation?
   Ⓐ April Ⓒ June
   Ⓑ May Ⓓ July

2. During which month does Cheyenne receive the least precipitation?
   Ⓐ January Ⓒ October
   Ⓑ February Ⓓ November

3. During which month does Cheyenne have the hottest average temperature?
   Ⓐ June Ⓒ August
   Ⓑ July Ⓓ September

4. During which month does Cheyenne have the coolest average temperature?
   Ⓐ January Ⓒ March
   Ⓑ February Ⓓ December

5. During which of these two months does Cheyenne receive the same amount of precipitation?
   Ⓐ March and October
   Ⓑ February and November
   Ⓒ May and July
   Ⓓ April and June

6. What is the average monthly precipitation in Cheyenne in March?
   Ⓐ 0.5 inch Ⓒ 1.5 inches
   Ⓑ 1 inch Ⓓ 2.0 inches

7. What is the average monthly precipitation in Cheyenne in September?
   Ⓐ 1.0 inch Ⓒ 1.5 inches
   Ⓑ 1.2 inches Ⓓ 1.7 inches

8. What is the average monthly temperature in Cheyenne in November?
   Ⓐ 1.75 degrees Ⓒ 30 degrees
   Ⓑ 25 degrees Ⓓ 35 degrees

Write a complete sentence to answer the question.

9. Using precipitation as a guide, what kind of climate do you think Cheyenne might have?

____

____

____

LESSON 3

Charts and Time Lines

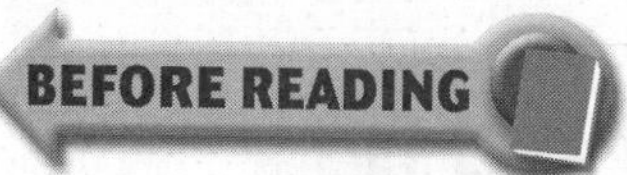

Tap Prior Knowledge

"Tidal Ranges": Ask the students if they have ever been the beach at low tide. How was the beach at low tide different from the beach at high tide?

"TV Ratings and Share": Ask the students if they have ever had a favorite TV show that was canceled. Why was the show canceled? How are ratings figured?

"Reading a Stock Market Report": Ask if any of the students own stock in a company. Where are shares of stock sold? Why do people buy stock?

"Time Line: 1860–1960": Ask the students if they know when important events happened in their family. If so, they could make a time line of those events. A time line is graphical organizer that shows the relationship between events in time.

Skill to Emphasize

Review the section about charts and time lines on page 5. Point out the charts and time line in the selections.

Preview Text Features

Point out the charts and the information they give or ask for. The chart in "Tidal Ranges" gives average tidal readings around the United States. The chart in "TV Ratings and Share" allows the students to calculate ratings and share and to show the relationships on a week-to-week basis. The stock report in "Reading a Stock Market Report" gives much information, and the specific meaning of each column of information should be discussed. Point out the time line in "Time Line: 1860–1960" and the sequential order of years and events. Boldfaced words indicate vocabulary words.

Comprehending the Selection

Ask the students: *What does the chart show?* or *What does the time line show?* Ask the students how the visual aid helps them to learn more about the topic.

Reinforce the Comprehension Skill

Remind the students that charts and time lines organize information in an easy-to-understand format. Ask the students if they think charts and time lines are a good way to show information. Ask them what other kinds of charts they might have used that day.

Assess

Have the students complete the activities for each selection.

SELECTION DETAILS

Summary

"Tidal Ranges" (page 15): A chart points out varying average tidal ranges around the United States.

"TV Ratings and Share" (page 16): This article explains how TV ratings and share are figured.

"Reading a Stock Market Report" (page 17): The article gives practice gleaning information from a stock market report.

"Time Line: 1860–1960" (page 18): The time line details some of the key historical events in Arizona between 1860 and 1960.

Selection Type

Science Article
Social Studies Articles

Comprehension Skill

Use Visual Aids for Information

Standards

Reading

- Use a variety of appropriate reference materials, including representations of information such as diagrams, maps, and charts, to gather information.

Science

- Describe the movement of water on the Earth.

Social Studies

- Construct and interpret graphs and charts using historical data.
- Understand the role of entrepreneurs in the free enterprise system who take the risks of organizing productive resources.
- Put in chronological order important events in major study units.

VOCABULARY

"TV Ratings and Share"
ratings *share*

"Reading a Stock Market Report"
stock market *shares of stock*
stockholder *dividend*

Name ______________________________ Date ______________

Tidal Ranges

The difference between the average high tide and the average low tide is called the average tidal range. Because of the varying shapes of the coastlines, different places have different average tidal ranges. Read the chart. It shows the average tidal ranges for different places in the United States.

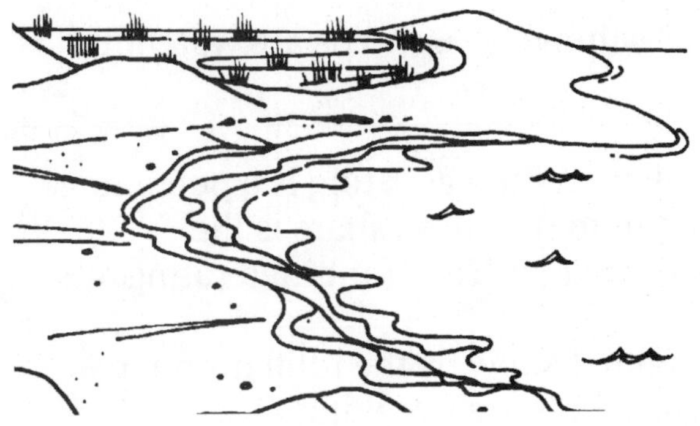

PLACE	AVERAGE TIDAL RANGE IN METERS
Portland, Maine	2.7
Boston, Massachusetts	2.9
New York City, New York	1.4
Savannah, Georgia	2.2
Key West, Florida	0.4
Galveston, Texas	0.4
San Diego, California	1.2
San Francisco, California	1.2
Seattle, Washington	2.3
Cordova, Alaska	3.0
Honolulu, Hawaii	0.4

Read the selection. Then, use the chart and write complete sentences to answer the questions.

1. Which place on the chart has the highest average tidal range?

____

2. Which place has a higher average tidal range: Portland, Maine, or Seattle, Washington?

____

3. Which three places have the same average tidal range?

____

4. What is the average tidal range in Savannah, Georgia?

____

5. What is the difference between the highest average tidal range and the lowest average tidal range on the chart?

____

Name ______________________ Date__________

TV Ratings and Share

When a television show you like is canceled, it is probably because of that show's **ratings**. Ratings are an estimate of how many people watch a given show. They are actually a percentage shown to the first decimal place. A typical rating for a prime-time show would be 15.7. Over 99 million U.S. households have televisions. Because there are so many televisions, a special sample is made by using electronic equipment. This sample involves 5,000 households.

To find a show's rating, divide the number watching that show by the total number of sample households. For example, if 525 households are watching the show, you would divide 525 by 5,000 to get 0.105 or 10.5% or a rating of 10.5.

1. If a show has a 15.7 rating, how many of the 5,000 sample households are watching?

____

There is another factor besides rating. It is called **share**. Whereas rating is a percentage of all the households that have televisions that are tuned in to the show, share is the percentage of households that have their televisions turned on. The combined rating and share would look like 15.7/30.

To find a show's share, divide the number watching that show by the total number watching something. For example, suppose 2,500 households are watching TV and 950 households are watching a particular show. You would divide the number watching that particular show by the total number watching something, or 950 divided by 2,500 equals .038 or 38% or a 38 share.

2. The chart below gives information for three separate weeks of television viewing for the 5,000 sample households for three programs. Complete the ratings and share portions. Assume that these are the only three shows on in this time-slot.

	WEEK ONE			WEEK TWO			WEEK THREE		
	Watching	Rating	Share	Watching	Rating	Share	Watching	Rating	Share
Dumb Dog	794			735			735		
Time Warp	1,009			779			979		
Winnie's Wanders	621			706			756		

 **Write complete sentences to answer the questions.**

3. Why did *Dumb Dog* have the same share in Week One and Week Two, but have different ratings?

____

4. Which show's rating increased, even though its share decreased?

____

____

Name ______________________________ Date ______________

Reading a Stock Market Report

In the **stock market**, people buy and sell **shares of stock** in companies. People put their money into companies by buying shares of stock. A **stockholder** owns part of a company. The size of the part depends on the number of shares the stockholder owns. The stock market report below shows information about six different companies. Each company usually has an abbreviated name on the stock report. Sometimes a stock pays a **dividend**, or an amount of money each quarter. The amounts, other than sales, are in dollars.

52-week		Stock	Dividend	Sales 100s	High of the Day	Low of the Day	Last of the Day	Change in Price
High	Low							
$68\frac{1}{2}$	$55\frac{1}{2}$	Toxaco	3.20	9687	$61\frac{3}{8}$	$60\frac{1}{8}$	61	$+1\frac{1}{2}$
$39\frac{3}{8}$	$21\frac{1}{4}$	TmMir	1.08	2034	$31\frac{1}{2}$	$30\frac{3}{8}$	$31\frac{1}{2}$	$+\frac{3}{4}$
$37\frac{1}{2}$	$27\frac{1}{8}$	USV	1.40	10934	$31\frac{1}{8}$	$30\frac{1}{2}$	$30\frac{1}{2}$	$+\frac{1}{8}$
$44\frac{5}{8}$	33	Downjohn	1.16	10578	$42\frac{1}{4}$	$41\frac{3}{8}$	42	$-\frac{1}{4}$
32	20	Woolgrns	0.46	4192	$32\frac{3}{8}$	$31\frac{7}{8}$	$32\frac{7}{8}$	$+1\frac{1}{4}$
24	$13\frac{3}{4}$	Wynds	0.60	17	$18\frac{1}{2}$	18	18	$-\frac{1}{2}$

Study the report. Then answer the questions.

1. What was the highest price paid for USV stock in the last year?

____

2. What was the lowest price paid for Downjohn stock on this day?

____

3. Which stock showed the largest change in price from one day to the next?

____

4. Which stock shown paid the highest dividend?

____

5. What dividend was paid by Woolgrns per share?

____

6. If a person owned 1,000 shares of Toxaco, how much dividend was that person paid?

____

7. How many 100s of shares of Wynds stock were sold?

____

Name ______________________ Date ____________

Time Line: 1860–1960

A time line shows the order of events in a certain period of time. The events and time they happen are presented along a vertical or horizontal line. This line shows the sequence of events. The time line below shows important events in Arizona history from 1860 to 1960.

Time Line of Arizona History from 1860–1960

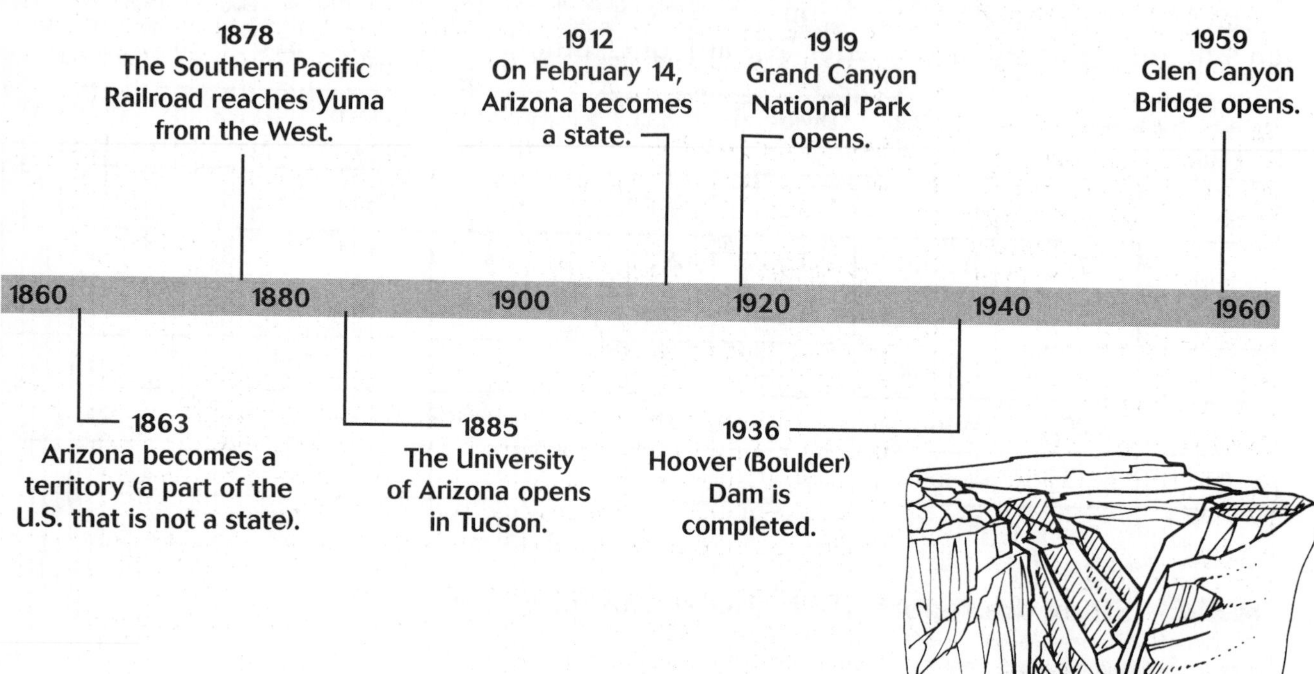
1878
The Southern Pacific Railroad reaches Yuma from the West.
1912
On February 14, Arizona becomes a state.
1919
Grand Canyon National Park opens.
1959
Glen Canyon Bridge opens.
1860
1880
1900
1920
1940
1960
1863
Arizona becomes a territory (a part of the U.S. that is not a state).
1885
The University of Arizona opens in Tucson.
1936
Hoover (Boulder) Dam is completed.

Use the time line to answer the questions. Darken the circle by the best answer.

1. The University of Arizona opened in Tucson in _____.
   Ⓐ 1878
   Ⓑ 1880
   Ⓒ 1885
   Ⓓ 1888

2. The _____ reached Yuma in 1878.
   Ⓐ Grand Canyon
   Ⓑ University of Tucson
   Ⓒ Glen Canyon Bridge
   Ⓓ Southern Pacific Railroad

3. Before Arizona became a state, _____.
   Ⓐ Grand Canyon National Park opened
   Ⓑ Arizona became a territory
   Ⓒ Hoover Dam was completed
   Ⓓ Glen Canyon Bridge opened

4. After Grand Canyon National Park opened, _____.
   Ⓐ the University of Arizona opened
   Ⓑ Arizona became a state
   Ⓒ Hoover Dam was completed
   Ⓓ the Southern Pacific Railroad reached Yuma

Maps

Tap Prior Knowledge

"The Middle East": Ask the students if they have ever used a map to learn more about a place. Do they know where the Middle East is? What do they know about the Middle East and its people and history?

"Animal Migration": Ask the students if they have ever seen geese flying north or south in migration. Why do animals migrate?

"Reading a Landform Map": Ask the students to identify various kinds of landforms. What kinds of natural regions do they know about? What landforms and natural regions are present in their area?

Skill to Emphasize

Review the section about maps on page 5. Point out the maps in the selections.

Preview Text Features

Point out the title of the map in each article. Point out the compass rose on each map. Have the students name the four cardinal directions: north, south, east, and west. Ask them if they know the intermediate directions of northeast, northwest, southeast, and southwest. Point out the map key in the Middle East map and the shading used to designate the Fertile Crescent. Point out the map key in the migration map and the shading used to designate different biomes. Boldfaced words indicate vocabulary words.

Comprehending the Selection

Ask the students: *What does the map show?* Ask the students how the map helps them to learn more about the place.

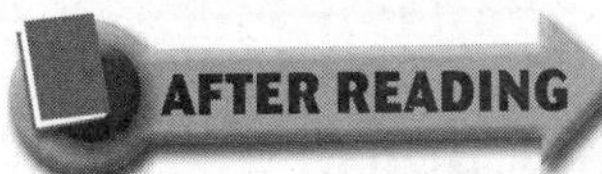

Reinforce the Comprehension Skill

Remind the students that a map gives information about a place. Ask the students if they think maps are a good way to show information. Ask them what other kinds of maps they might have used that day, such as a weather map.

Assess

Have the students complete the activities for the selection.

Have the students do research on landforms in their state. Then, have the students draw an outline map of their state; they should include a title and a map key that uses a symbol for each landform. Finally, they should shade in the areas of the state in which those landforms are found.

Have the students search through the newspaper or news magazines for maps. Have them bring these maps to school to share with the class. Discuss what information the maps show.

SELECTION DETAILS

Summary

"The Middle East" (page 20): This map gives the political boundaries of nations in the Middle East and points out the historical region called the Fertile Crescent.
"Animal Migration" (page 21): This article includes a map showing the migration paths of three animals.
"Reading a Landform Map" (page 22): This map shows the major landforms and natural regions of the Southwest Region of the United States.

Selection Type

Science Article
Social Studies Articles

Comprehension Skill

Use Visual Aids for Information

Standards

Reading
- Use a variety of appropriate reference materials, including representations of information such as diagrams, maps, and charts, to gather information.

Science
- Explain the behavior of living/nonliving components in an ecosystem.

Social Studies
- Understand map keys showing boundaries, distance, physical features, and location.
- Use maps to identify physical and human features of North America.

VOCABULARY

"The Middle East"
political map, Fertile Crescent

"Reading a Landform Map"
population map, precipitation map, resource map, landform map

Name ______________________________ Date ______________

The Middle East

A **political map** shows the boundaries of nations. Often, the capital city and major cities of a nation are included on a political map. The map below shows the Middle East today. It also includes information on a historical region called the **Fertile Crescent**. Notice the compass rose, map key, and distance scale on the map.

THE MIDDLE EAST

THE MIDDLE EAST
TURKEY
Tigris River
Mediterranean Sea
Teheran
Beirut
SYRIA
LEBANON
Damascus
Baghdad
Jerusalem
IRAQ
ISRAEL
Amman
IRAN
Euphrates River
Cairo
Kuwait City
JORDAN
KUWAIT
EGYPT
BAHRAIN
Doha
Abu Dhabi
Riyadh
SAUDI ARABIA
QATAR
Muscat
UNITED ARAB EMIRATES
OMAN
N
W
E
S
Red Sea
SUDAN
Indian Ocean
Sana
Khartoum
YEMEN
0 400 Mi
0 200 400 600 Km
Map Key
Fertile Crescent
National capital
Rivers

Use the map to answer the questions.

1. Which city is the capital of Sudan? ______________________________

2. What body of water forms Saudi Arabia's western border?

   ____

3. Which city is nearer Baghdad: Kuwait City or Teheran? About how far in miles is the nearer city from Baghdad?

   ____

4. What is the distance in kilometers from Cairo to Amman? ______________________________

5. The Fertile Crescent was the location of several early civilizations. Between which two rivers was the Fertile Crescent located?

   ____

6. In which present-day countries is much of the Fertile Crescent located?

   ____

Name ______________________ Date ____________

Animal Migration

Many animals migrate long distances between their summer and winter homes. Migrating animals usually spend winters in the South and summers in the North. Some, especially birds, return to exactly the same spot year after year. Study the map below about migrating animals.

Migration Paths of Three Animals

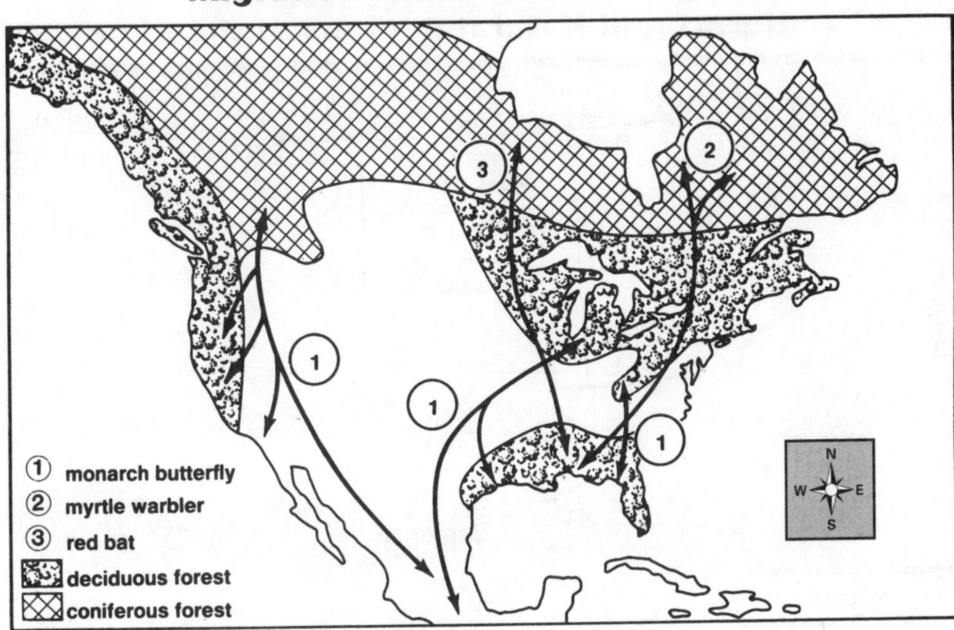

Use the map to answer the questions. Write complete sentences.

1. Between what two biomes does the red bat migrate? ______________________

2. Which animal has more than one migratory route? ______________________

3. Which two animals migrate between the same two biomes? ______________________

4. In what type of biome does the myrtle warbler spend the winter? ______________________

5. Why do you think some animals migrate?

Name ______________________ Date ____________

Reading a Landform Map

Maps can give many kinds of information about a place. A **population map** shows how many people live in an area. A **precipitation map** shows how much rain or rain and snow an area gets each year. A **resource map** tells what kind of natural resources are found in an area. The map below is a **landform map**. It gives information about landforms and natural regions in the southwest part of the United States.

Major Landforms and Natural Regions of the Southwest

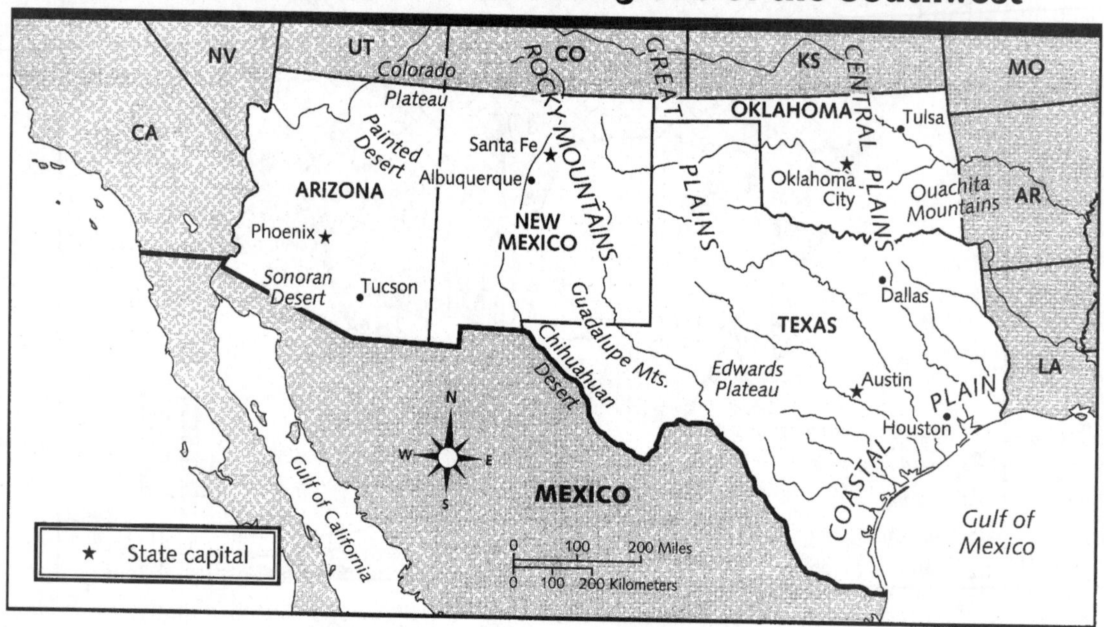

1. Which state in this region is farthest south?
   Ⓐ Arizona
   Ⓑ New Mexico
   Ⓒ Oklahoma
   Ⓓ Texas

2. What mountain range can be found in southeast Oklahoma?
   Ⓐ Rocky Mountains
   Ⓑ Ouachita Mountains
   Ⓒ Appalachian Mountains
   Ⓓ Guadalupe Mountains

3. In which natural region is Houston located?
   Ⓐ Colorado Plateau
   Ⓑ Great Plains
   Ⓒ Coastal Plain
   Ⓓ Chihuahuan Desert

4. Which desert can be found in Arizona?
   Ⓐ Sahara Desert
   Ⓑ Chihuahuan Desert
   Ⓒ Gobi Desert
   Ⓓ Painted Desert

Write complete sentences to answer the question.

5. Which state in this region probably has the most agricultural activity? Explain.

____

____

UNIT 2 Main Idea and Details

Nonfiction articles, for the most part, deal with facts. Writing that gives only facts is called informative writing. The writer provides details about who, what, when, where, or how. The reader of factual writing must first be concerned with details, the facts of the article.

Sometimes the writer will also ask why and then answer this question by drawing conclusions based on the facts. This kind of writing is called interpretive writing. Sometimes the reader must interpret, too. The reader may have to identify the main idea.

Main Idea (Lesson 5)

The main idea is the main point the writer is trying to make in the article. The main idea is not always stated directly in the article. How do readers decide what the main idea of an article is? First, they have to identify the topic of the article. The main idea will be some specific comment the writer is making about the topic. Usually, each paragraph has a main idea or topic sentence. Readers can put the topic sentences together to find the main idea of the article.

The main idea cannot be a statement not supported by the article. The main idea cannot be a statement that is only a detail.

To find the main idea of an article:

- Use the Main Idea Map on page 118.
- Read the article carefully.
- Find the topic of the article.
- Decide what all the sentences say about the topic.
- Ask yourself, "What is this article mostly about?"
- The title often gives a clue about the main idea.
- The main idea may be stated in the first paragraph.
- Write and revise the main idea.

Details (Lesson 6)

Details are facts that tell who, what, when, where, and how about a topic. Details add information to a story and make it more interesting. They should always support the main idea. To show their comprehension, readers are often asked to remember details from an article.

By reading carefully, readers can remember more details. By remembering more details, readers can more easily determine the main idea.

To recall specific facts and details:

- Use the Main Idea Map on page 118.
- Read the article carefully.
- Try to answer who, what, when, where, and how about the topic of the article.
- Reread the article if necessary to answer the question.

Summary (Lesson 7)

A summary is a short account of the main idea and key details of an article. A summary should include only the most important points in an article. Key details from the beginning, middle, and end of the article should be included. Readers must sometimes summarize an article when they need to condense the information in an article.

The ability to write a good summary shows the reader's comprehension of the article's main idea and key details.

To summarize an article:

- Use the Summary Chart on page 119.
- Read the article carefully, then put it aside.
- Think about the main idea and important details.
- Write the summary without looking at the article.
- Include only the main idea and important details.
- Do include the author's name (if given) and the title of the article.
- Do not use sentences, phrases, or direct quotes from the article.
- Do not use minor details, explanations, or examples.

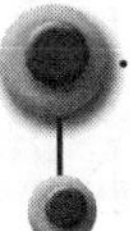

Graphic Organizers

Main Idea Web	page 118
Summary Chart	page 119

Research Base

"Content literacy involves knowing what to expect—anticipating the kinds of organizational structures the reader might encounter. Content literacy also involves understanding the kinds of graphic features the reader need to interpret, as well as vocabulary specific to the topic. The reader uses the text's organization. language, and visual features in a unified way to derive meaning. In other words students must learn how to read history, biology, environmental science, geographical descriptions, and other kinds of texts." (*Guiding Readers and Writers: Grades 3–6*, p. 400)

Main Idea

Tap Prior Knowledge

"By Jove! That's Where It Came From!": Ask the students if they know the origins of the words they use, such as the days of the week or the names of the months.

"Let's Go Surfing!": Ask the students if they like the beach. What about the beach do they like best? Have they ever surfed? Do they know how surfing has changed over time?

Skill to Emphasize

Review the section about main idea on page 23. Tell the students that they will try to find what each selection is mostly about. Have the students do the practice paragraphs before they move on to the other selections.

Preview Text Features

Each paragraph has a topic sentence. Point out the topic sentence in each paragraph of the two selections. Tell the students that if they think about all the topic sentences, they should be able to determine the main idea of each selection more easily. Subtitles tell what is in each section of the article. Diagrams help present concepts such as the changes in the size of surfboards. Boldfaced words indicate vocabulary words.

Comprehending the Selection

Model how to identify the main idea by asking: *What is this story mostly about?*

Reinforce the Comprehension Skill

Tell the students that the title of the selection often includes the topic. The main idea is some point about the topic. What is the author saying about surfing, for example? (that surfing is a fun activity that has changed over time)

Distribute copies of the Main Idea Map on page 118. Have the students complete the map for the two reading selections.

Assess

Have the students complete the activities for the selection.

Have the students do research on the origin of a word. Often dictionaries give some information on word origins. Then have the students write a paragraph telling what they have learned.

Have the students look for articles about surfing in the newspaper or magazines. Have them bring these articles to school to share with the class.

SELECTION DETAILS

Summary

"Find the Main Idea" (sample paragraphs, page 25): The sample paragraphs give practice in identifying the main idea in short selections.

"By Jove! That's Where It Came From!" (page 27): This article discusses words that originated from the names of Roman and Greek gods and goddesses.

"Let's Go Surfing!" (page 29): This article discusses the changes in the sport of surfing and in the shape and size of surfboards.

Selection Type

Language Arts Article
Social Studies Article

Comprehension Skill

Identify Main Idea

Standards

Reading

- Identify main idea and details.
- Determine the meaning of vocabulary using linguistic roots.

Social Studies

- Explain the effects of interactions between human and natural systems.

VOCABULARY

Introduce the vocabulary words. Write the words on the board. Help students find a definition for each word. Have students use each word in a sentence.

"By Jove! That's Where It Came From!"

agriculture	*martial*
military	*mercurial*

"Let's Go Surfing!"

envelop	*circuit*
maneuver	*eliminate*
cresting	*identity*
prolonging	*transformed*
array	*precise*

Name ________________________________ Date ____________

Find the Main Idea

Read each paragraph. Identify what it is mainly about. Darken the circle by the best answer.

People sometimes think that Native Americans lived only by hunting, but this isn't so. They also got food by fishing and farming, as well as by gathering wild grains, nuts, and roots. Native Americans who lived near the water ate shellfish and other fish. In some places people still find large piles of shells that were left by the Native Americans who once lived there.

1. This paragraph is mainly about _____.
   - Ⓐ eating shellfish
   - Ⓑ fishing and farming
   - Ⓒ gathering grains
   - Ⓓ foods that Native Americans ate

Salt was very valuable in ancient Rome. Roman soldiers were given an allowance of salt known as a salarium. The word *salary* comes from the Roman word for salt.

2. This paragraph is mainly about _____.
   - Ⓐ ancient Rome
   - Ⓑ where the word *salary* comes from
   - Ⓒ the value of salt
   - Ⓓ paying Roman soldiers

Frédéric-Auguste Bartholdi, the sculptor who designed the Statue of Liberty, began his career as a painter. He was 18 when he received his first commission for a public monument. The statue he designed was 12 feet tall. It was moved out of his studio with only one inch to spare. That statue established his reputation as a sculptor. It led to more commissions for oversized patriotic works.

3. This main idea of this paragraph is that _____.
   - Ⓐ Bartholdi was a good painter
   - Ⓑ only young men can do large sculptures
   - Ⓒ Bartholdi was always famous
   - Ⓓ Bartholdi created many huge sculptures

Voters do not elect the President of the United States. The Electoral College elects the President. At the end of Election Day, each state sends a number of electors to the Electoral College. The electors usually vote for the person who got the majority of votes in each state, but they are not required to do so.

4. This story is mainly about _____.
   - Ⓐ who really elects the President of the United States
   - Ⓑ graduating from the Electoral College
   - Ⓒ how electors get their job
   - Ⓓ after Election Day

Name ______________________________ Date ____________

Read each paragraph. Identify what it is mainly about. Darken the circle by the phrase or title that tells the main idea of the paragraph.

America probably could not have won its freedom from the British during the American Revolution without the help of the French. France provided arms, ships, money, and men to the American colonies. Some Frenchmen even became high-ranking officers in the American army. One of these men was the Marquis de Lafayette, a close friend of George Washington's.

5. What is the main idea of this paragraph?
   - Ⓐ George Washington's friend
   - Ⓑ The American colonies
   - Ⓒ How the French helped the Americans
   - Ⓓ The American Revolution

From the earliest colonial days, regulation and inspection of immigrants were the responsibilities of each individual state. The first federal immigration law wasn't enacted until 1819. The states' greatest fear was that immigrants would bring the dreaded diseases of smallpox, typhoid fever, and cholera with them. Screening of new immigrants focused almost completely on quarantine. As the immigrants disembarked at a port, a health inspector quickly scanned them for signs of contagious diseases. In New York, immigrants who were thought to have any of these diseases were sent to Marine Hospital on Staten Island.

6. What is the main idea of this paragraph?
   - Ⓐ Reasons for screening immigrants
   - Ⓑ Contagious diseases
   - Ⓒ The first federal immigration law
   - Ⓓ Where immigrants were sent

During the 1800s, the number of immigrants to America increased rapidly, from 150,000 during the 1820s, to 1.7 million in the 1840s, and to 2.5 million in the 1850s. The 1800s are often referred to as the first wave of immigration to the United States. Three catastrophic events were the main reasons behind it—the end of the Napoleonic Wars in 1815, the potato famines of the 1840s in Ireland, and the change in economic conditions in Europe caused by the Industrial Revolution.

7. What is the main idea of this paragraph?
   - Ⓐ Three catastrophic events that occurred
   - Ⓑ All about the Industrial Revolution
   - Ⓒ Why immigration to America increased in the 1800s
   - Ⓓ None of the above

Horses today look very different than their ancestors. The first horses were not much larger than rabbits. They lived in forests and were called Eohippus, or Dawn Horse, because they lived at the beginning of the Age of Mammals. The Dawn Horse had four toes on each front foot and three toes on each hind foot. Horses today have only one toe on both front and hind legs. The hoof is actually the nail of that toe.

8. What is the main idea of this paragraph?
   - Ⓐ How many toes horse have
   - Ⓑ How horses have changed
   - Ⓒ The age of mammals
   - Ⓓ Dawn Horses of the forest

Name ______________________ Date __________

By Jove! That's Where It Came From!

Many words that we use every day came from the names of Roman or Greek gods or goddesses. Many of the planets are named for Roman gods or goddesses. Venus is named for the Roman goddess of gardens, and Saturn is named for the Roman god of **agriculture**. Pluto is named for the Roman god of the underworld, and Neptune is named for the Roman god of water. Some of the months, such as June (for Juno), are named for gods or goddesses, too.

Jove, the chief Roman god (who was also known as Jupiter), had many sons. He was thought of as being cheerful and hearty. Today when we describe someone as being cheerful, we say that person is very *jovial*. Jove also had a sister named Ceres. She was the Roman goddess of agriculture. The word *cereal* comes from her name.

Mars is the name of a planet and of a famous son of the god Jove. Mars was the Roman god of war, so when we speak of **military** things, we often use the word ***martial***. When we talk about people who might live on the planet Mars, we call them *Martians*. The month of March is named for Mars.

January is named for Janus, another son of Jove. Janus was the Roman god of doorways and bridges. He had two faces, one in front, looking ahead, and one in back, looking to the past. Perhaps the month of January was named for Janus because it comes after the old year and at the beginning of the new year.

Another son of Jove was Mercury. Mercury is the name of the metallic element Hg, the only liquid metal. Mercury is also the name of a planet. Mercury was a very speedy messenger when he delivered the messages of the Roman gods and goddesses. The messages were always delivered to different places or positions in time. When we speak of people who move about quickly and are always changing, we call them ***mercurial***.

Pan was the Greek god of the woods and forests. He is usually shown as being half man and half goat. It was believed that Pan lived in places where people did not go. Sometimes when people are alone in nature or new situations, they become frightened. The words used to describe this feeling are *panic* and *panicky*.

Name ______________________________ Date____________

Comprehension and Vocabulary Review

Darken the circle by the best answer.

1. Pluto is named for the Roman god of _____.
   Ⓐ war
   Ⓑ water
   Ⓒ the underworld
   Ⓓ agriculture

2. What is the main idea of this selection?
   Ⓐ to tell about Jove and his sons
   Ⓑ to tell about planets that are named for Roman gods and goddesses
   Ⓒ to tell how some words became part of our language
   Ⓓ to teach about Roman and Greek mythology

3. The metal mercury is also called quicksilver. How is the god Mercury like the metal mercury?
   Ⓐ He is fast.
   Ⓑ He is Jove's son.
   Ⓒ He has a famous brother.
   Ⓓ He likes to deliver messages.

4. Why does the author compare the god Janus to the month of January?
   Ⓐ January is a cold month.
   Ⓑ January faces the old and the new.
   Ⓒ Janus was Jove's first son.
   Ⓓ Janus was the brother of Mars.

5. If someone you know likes to have fun, you might say that person is most like _____.
   Ⓐ Janus
   Ⓑ Pan
   Ⓒ Mars
   Ⓓ Jove

6. A person who is frightened about a new situation is _____.
   Ⓐ martial
   Ⓑ panicky
   Ⓒ cereal
   Ⓓ mercurial

7. Which of these could be another title for this article?
   Ⓐ Words We Get from Mythology
   Ⓑ Jove and His Sons
   Ⓒ Roman Gods and Their Planets
   Ⓓ The Martians Are Coming

8. What can you conclude about the author of this article?
   Ⓐ He believes you should always use the dictionary.
   Ⓑ He believes that everyone should study mythology.
   Ⓒ He is interested in studying the origin of words.
   Ⓓ He knows everything about the planets.

Answer the question below in complete sentences.

9. Do you think it is a good idea to know the origins of words? Why or why not?

____

____

____

____

Name ______________________________ Date ____________

Let's Go Surfing!

Imagine yourself a hundred yards from a glittering sandy beach. Brilliant sunshine fills a crystal clear sky and warms your back. Light dances off the water that surrounds you. You're racing toward the shore at close to 50 miles (80 kilometers) per hour. There is only a thin board beneath your feet to separate you from the powerful ocean. A towering wave threatens to **envelop** you, but you stay just ahead of it. Shifting your weight from one foot to the other, you **maneuver** the board through the smooth water below the **cresting** wave. Hey, hey! You're surfing!

Riding the Waves

Surfing is a water sport performed mostly in the ocean, although some committed surfers try to find waves in large lakes. Surfers use rigid boards to glide across the smooth sloping parts of waves. First, they lie on the boards to paddle out beyond the breaking waves. Then, surfers turn to face the beach. Next, they kneel on the boards. Finally, they stand as the wave begins to rise. Surfers ride the wave toward the shore, **prolonging** the ride by moving across the face of the wave.

Skilled surfers use balance and timing to perform an **array** of different tricks. Today's surfers show their skills in two main ways. One type of surfer participates in organized competitions. Judges rank tricks, length of ride, and even grace while riding. This competitive surfing has been accepted by the International Olympic Committee.

Another type of surfer views the sport as a purely personal way to get close to nature. These surfers avoid the competition **circuit** and search the globe for the perfect wave to enjoy in private. You may not be able to admire these surfers' moves in competition, but you can often find videos or magazines that showcase their skills.

Name ______________________________ Date______________

Surfer Lingo

360: a trick where the surfer does a complete turn

hang ten: a trick where all ten toes rest on the nose of the surfboard

ono: Hawaiian word for "great"

ripping: doing amazing tricks on a wave

wipe out: when a surfer is knocked off a surfboard by a wave

the zone: area inside or between waves when they are breaking

A Royal History

Surfing traces its history to the early Polynesians, including those living in what is now Hawaii. Some experts believe that Hawaiian kings surfed in their religious ceremonies. Others say that both kings and citizens enjoyed surfing as a sport. In any case, early surfing dates back at least to the 15th century. Change came in the 1800s, however, when large numbers of Europeans arrived in Hawaii. Some Europeans did not like the sport and tried to **eliminate** it.

Duke Kahanamoku

In 1920, however, a young Hawaiian named Duke Kahanamoku helped bring the sport back by founding a surfing club. Duke was no ordinary Hawaiian. He was an Olympic swimming champion, grandson of a high chief, and an accomplished surfer. Duke gained recognition for his sport by traveling as far away as Australia to show off his skills. Surfing also grew in popularity as more and more people visited Hawaii for its sunny weather and lovely beaches. These tourists brought news of surfing back to the mainland.

Then, during the 1950s and 1960s, the **identity** of the surfer began to change. Surfers developed their own language. You could spot surfers by their suntans and the casual clothes they wore. Before long, surf music and movies helped bring surfing style to young people all over the United States.

Name ______________________________ Date ____________

The Changing Surfboard

The early Hawaiians surfed on wooden boards that were 18 feet (5.5 meters) long. Duke Kahanamoku's boards were 8 to 10 feet (2.4 to 3 meters) long and solid wood. These surfboards were heavy and hard to handle.

However, over time, surfboards improved. In the 1930s, a surfer looking for speed developed a hollow board. The surfer also added a fin to help him guide the board. Even this board still weighed 60 to 70 pounds (27.2 to 31.8 kilograms)!

It wasn't long before lighter woods and plastics led to the *malibu*, a board weighing just 20 pounds (9 kilograms). The malibu **transformed** surfing. Now surfers could really steer their boards. They could move around to do tricks. Even carrying a surfboard became much easier. This encouraged surfers to travel in search of "perfect" waves. Most of all, malibus made learning to surf easier. This brought more and more people to the sport.

Today's surfboards are very different from those used by the first surfers. The new boards are built mostly of plastic. They are shorter and usually more narrow than the early boards. A typical board is now about 6 feet (1.8 meters) long and weighs about 5 pounds (2.3 kilograms). Also, most boards now have three fins as well as shaped edges to make steering more **precise**. If you ever take to the waves, you'll enjoy these improvements. They'll keep you ahead of that huge wave.

Surfboards Then and Now

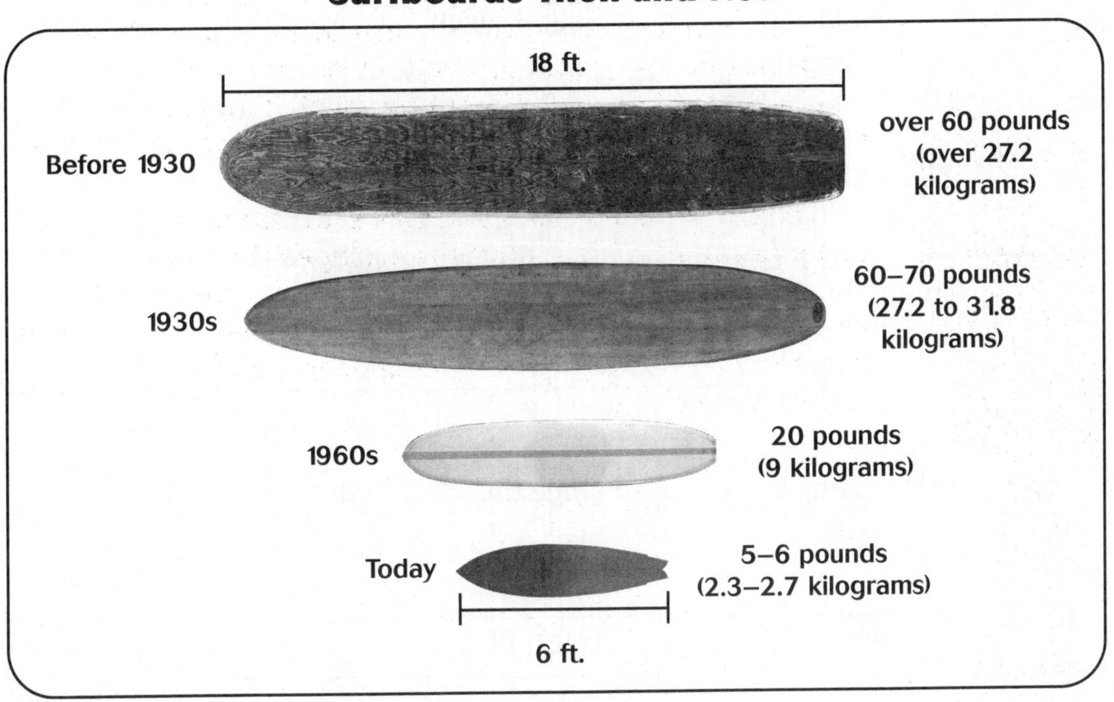

Name ______________________________ Date ______________

Comprehension Review

Darken the circle by the best answer.

1. A surfer rides a _____ across the face of a wave.
   Ⓐ bicycle
   Ⓑ boat
   Ⓒ board
   Ⓓ train

2. What do surfers do after turning to face the beach?
   Ⓐ Lie on their boards.
   Ⓑ Kneel and stand up.
   Ⓒ Paddle beyond the waves.
   Ⓓ Turn on their video cameras.

3. What is the main idea of this article?
   Ⓐ Some Europeans tried to eliminate surfing.
   Ⓑ Early surfboards were very heavy.
   Ⓒ Surfing has changed over the years.
   Ⓓ Duke Kahanamoku swam in the Olympics.

4. Under which subhead would you most likely find information about surfboards used in the 1930s?
   Ⓐ Riding the Waves
   Ⓑ The Changing Surfboard
   Ⓒ Surfer Talk
   Ⓓ A Royal History

5. What changed about surfing because of the malibu?
   Ⓐ Competition became tougher.
   Ⓑ Surf clothing became unavailable.
   Ⓒ Surfers could steer better.
   Ⓓ Boards became heavier.

6. In which U.S. city do you think a surfer would most likely live?
   Ⓐ San Diego, California
   Ⓑ Dallas, Texas
   Ⓒ Denver, Colorado
   Ⓓ Kansas City, Missouri

Answer the questions below in complete sentences.

7. Identify two basic types of surfers. How are they similar and different?

____

____

____

8. What are two ways that surfing has changed since the 15th century?

____

____

____

Name ______________________________ Date ______________

Vocabulary Review

 **Use the words in the box to complete the paragraph.**

circuit	**eliminate**	**envelop**	**transformed**

As the fog begins to ______________ (1) the beach, the lone surfer can hardly see his way to the shore. When the Sun rises, the heat will ______________ (2) the fog, and he will feel warmer. By noon, the once-quiet beach will be ______________ (3) by a crowd of noisy surfers. The competition ______________ (4) has added the lone surfer's favorite beach to its list.

Build Your Vocabulary

Dictionaries give word spellings to help the reader with pronunciations. They also give definitions of the word.

Answer the first part of each item by writing a word from the box on the line. Answer the second part by circling the correct choice.

array	**cresting**	**identity**	**maneuver**	**precise**	**prolonging**

5. Write the correct spelling of (KREST ing). ______________
   It means— **a.** rising **b.** falling
6. Write the correct spelling of (pree SYSS). ______________
   It means— **a.** general **b.** exact
7. Write the correct spelling of (muh NOO vuhr). ______________
   It means— **a.** wander **b.** steer
8. Write the correct spelling of (pro LAWNG ing). ______________
   It means— **a.** lasting longer **b.** stopping suddenly
9. Write the correct spelling of (uh RAY). ______________
   It means— **a.** a selection **b.** just one choice
10. Write the correct spelling of (eye DEN tuh tee). ______________
    It means— **a.** who you are **b.** naming someone

Details

SELECTION DETAILS

Summary
"Find the Details" (sample paragraphs, page 35): The sample paragraphs give practice in identifying the details in short selections.

"Stormy Weather" (page 36): This article gives details on the causes of various weather events.

"Solar Eclipse" (page 37): This article gives details on the causes of a solar eclipse and how scientists study eclipses.

"Read a Food Label" (page 38): This article gives students practice in reading the details contained in food labels.

Selection Type
Science Articles

Comprehension Skill
Identify Details

Standards

Reading
- Identify main idea and supporting details.

Science
- Describe large-scale and local weather systems.
- Explain the relationship between common objects in the solar system.
- Demonstrate the ability to access accurate health information.

VOCABULARY

Introduce the vocabulary words. Write the words on the board. Help students find a definition for each word. Have students use each word in a sentence.

"Stormy Weather"
squall line *extensive*
torrential

"Solar Eclipse"
eclipse

Tap Prior Knowledge

"Stormy Weather": Ask the students if they have ever been caught in a thunderstorm. What caused the storm?

"Solar Eclipse": Ask the students if they have ever witnessed a solar or lunar eclipse. What caused the eclipse? What are some safety precautions associated with a solar eclipse?

"Read a Food Label": Ask the students if they have ever read a food label. What sort of information is displayed on a food label? Why are food labels important?

Skill to Emphasize

Review the section about details on page 23. Tell the students that they must pay attention to all the facts in the articles they read. Those facts are called details.

Preview Text Features

Each paragraph has a topic sentence. Point out the topic sentence in each paragraph. Each topic sentence is supported by detail sentences. The detail sentences give facts, or details, about the topic sentence. Boldfaced words indicate vocabulary words.

Comprehending the Selection

Model how to identify the details by asking: *What facts does the article tell about who, what, when, where, and how?*

Reinforce the Comprehension Skill

Tell the students that the main idea is the general point the author is making. Sometimes the main idea is suggested by the title. The details are specific facts that help the author to achieve the main idea. Ask the students to identify some of the details in the article.

Distribute copies of the Main Idea Map on page 118. Have the students complete the map for the "Stormy Weather" and "Solar Eclipse" articles.

Assess

Have the students complete the activities for the selections.

Have the students write a story about how they might feel if they were caught in a torrential rainstorm. What would they do?

AT HOME

Have the students search through the newspaper for an article about current events. Have the students list the important details of who, what, when, where, and how. Have the students bring their articles and lists to share with the class.

Name ________________________________ Date ____________

Find the Details

Details are small bits of information that answer the questions who, what, when, where, how much, or how many. Details support the main idea of a selection.

Read each selection. Darken the circle by the answer that best completes each sentence.

A muscle is made of fine threads called fibers. The fibers are held together by a fine, web-like connecting tissue. The muscle fibers can shorten and thicken when a message is sent to them through the nerves. When the fibers become shorter, the whole muscle becomes shorter. The shortening of the muscle is called a contraction. The lengthening of the muscle is known as relaxing. This process is how movements all over the body are produced.

1. Muscle threads are called _____.
   Ⓐ tissues
   Ⓑ webs
   Ⓒ fibers
   Ⓓ forearms

The spider is not an insect. A true insect has six legs, while a spider has eight. Also, the body of an insect is usually divided into three parts: head, chest, and abdomen. A spider's body is divided into only two parts, with the head and chest united. In certain species of spiders, the long legs have seven joints so the spider can move in any direction.

The spider's mouth contains fangs that are somewhat similar to the fangs in a snake's mouth. When a spider bites its prey, a drop of poison is injected into the blood of these small insects. The tiny amount of poison in most spiders is not enough to harm humans.

The spider has six spinning fingers called spinnerets. The liquid silk is manufactured inside the body of the spider. The liquid is forced through tiny holes in the ends of the spinnerets. When the silk is exposed to air, it hardens immediately.

2. An insect's body has _____.
   Ⓐ eight eyes
   Ⓑ three parts
   Ⓒ two parts
   Ⓓ long legs

3. A spider's mouth is similar to _____.
   Ⓐ an insect's mouth
   Ⓑ a cat's mouth
   Ⓒ a snake's mouth
   Ⓓ a silk covering

4. The spider preys on _____.
   Ⓐ spinnerets
   Ⓑ snakes
   Ⓒ small insects
   Ⓓ humans

5. The liquid silk comes through holes in _____.
   Ⓐ the fangs
   Ⓑ the spider's eggs
   Ⓒ the spinnerets
   Ⓓ the insect's body

Name ______________________ Date ____________

Stormy Weather

As warm, moist air rises, it almost always produces storms with dark clouds, high winds, and heavy precipitation. Some storms become severe, with thunder and lightning, a huge electric spark that travels from cloud to cloud or from clouds to the ground. Lightning can be dangerous if a person or an object is in its path. In some thunderstorms, hail forms as rain freezes in the clouds and forms ice. If the precipitation is heavy enough or lasts long enough, flooding can occur.

A line of violent thunderstorms, called a **squall line**, sometimes accompanies the passage of a cold front. Warm air rises rapidly in front of the advancing cold air, producing an area of very low pressure. Air rushes into the low-pressure area from all sides, resulting in a twisting, funnel-shaped storm called a tornado. The extremely high winds of a tornado can destroy almost everything in their path.

Over tropical oceans in summer months, conditions sometimes cause very warm, moist air to rise rapidly, forming a large, intense storm called a hurricane. A fully developed hurricane has bands of clouds spinning around a calm eye. As a hurricane nears land, strong winds, large waves, high tides, and **torrential** rains can cause **extensive** damage.

When cold air from the poles meets warm air from the tropics, a large spinning storm forms. In winter, these storms sometimes combine heavy snow and strong winds to produce a blizzard. Deep, drifting snow and bitter-cold temperatures make blizzards very dangerous.

Darken the circle by the answer that best completes each sentence.

1. Where warm and cold air masses meet, _____.
   Ⓐ it never rains
   Ⓑ a squall line may form
   Ⓒ a hurricane may form
   Ⓓ a lake forms

2. A line of violent thunderstorms is called a _____.
   Ⓐ rainbow
   Ⓑ vortex
   Ⓒ front
   Ⓓ squall line

3. A hurricane may develop in _____.
   Ⓐ a cold polar ocean
   Ⓑ a warm tropical ocean
   Ⓒ any ocean
   Ⓓ a tornado

4. A blizzard may develop where _____.
   Ⓐ a polar air mass meets a cold, moist air mass
   Ⓑ two warm air masses meet
   Ⓒ a polar air mass meets a warm, moist air mass
   Ⓓ two tornadoes meet

Name ______________________________ Date ____________

Solar Eclipse

An **eclipse** of the Sun is called a solar eclipse. During a solar eclipse, the Moon moves directly between the Earth and the Sun. The Moon shuts out the view of the Sun. The shadow of the Moon falls on the Earth.

A solar eclipse starts when the Moon begins to pass in front of the Sun. At first, it blocks only a small part of the Sun from view. Soon, almost the entire surface of the Sun is hidden. (This is called a total eclipse.) The daytime sky darkens. For a few minutes, it seems as if it is late evening. Then, more and more of the Sun becomes visible as the Moon continues to move. The eclipse ends when the Moon no longer blocks the Sun.

Scientists can learn much about the Sun during a solar eclipse. However, a total eclipse cannot be seen from any one spot for longer than 7 minutes and 40 seconds. That doesn't give the scientists much time to make their observations. So during a solar eclipse in 1973, a group of scientists took their equipment aboard a jet. The jet sped across the sky, all the time staying in the Moon's narrow shadow. These scientists were able to study a total eclipse for 74 minutes.

Darken the circle by the answer that best completes each sentence.

1. A total eclipse be seen from one place for only _____.
   - Ⓐ 1 minute
   - Ⓑ 1 hour
   - Ⓒ 74 minutes
   - Ⓓ 7 minutes and 40 seconds

2. During a solar eclipse, _____ falls on the Earth.
   - Ⓐ the Sun
   - Ⓑ the shadow of the Moon
   - Ⓒ a part of the space station
   - Ⓓ the sky

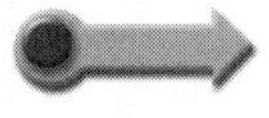

Write complete sentences to answer the questions.

3. What is a solar eclipse?

____

____

____

4. What causes a solar eclipse?

____

____

____

____

Name ______________________ Date ____________

Read a Food Label

The skill of observation is important when deciding what foods to eat. Food labels contain important information about the nutritional value of foods. To find out if a food is healthy for you, you should read its label carefully.

Read the cereal box label. Use it to answer the questions below.

1. How many calories are in one serving of this cereal without milk? With milk?

2. Does this cereal contain more carbohydrates or more fats?

3. Does this cereal contain more starch or more sugar?

4. What does *RDA* mean?

5. How much of the U.S. RDA of vitamin A is in $\frac{1}{4}$ cup of cereal?

6. What vitamins are in this cereal?

7. Which do you think are the five main ingredients in this cereal?

8. According to the cereal box, how could you increase the amount of protein in this cereal?

Each serving contains 4 g dietary fiber, including 1 g (2.6% by weight) non-nutritive crude fiber.

NUTRITION INFORMATION PER SERVING

Serving Size: 1/4 cup Raisin Bran (1 ounce bran flakes with 1/3 ounce raisins) alone, and in combination with 1/2 cup Vitamin D fortified whole milk.
Servings Per Container: 15

	Raisin Bran	
	1 oz. Cereal & 1/3 oz. raisins	with 1/2 cup whole milk
Calories	120	190
Protein	3 g	7 g
Carbohydrate	29 g	35 g
Fat	1 g	5 g

PERCENTAGE OF U.S. RECOMMENDED DAILY ALLOWANCE (U.S. RDA)

	Raisin Bran	
	1 oz. Cereal & 1/3 oz. raisins	with 1/2 cup whole milk
Protein	4	15
Vitamin A	25	30
Vitamin C	*	2
Thiamin	25	30
Riboflavin	25	35
Niacin	25	25
Calcium	*	15
Iron	25	25
Vitamin D	10	25
Vitamin B4	25	25
Folic Acid	25	25
Vitamin B12	25	30
Phosphorus	15	25
Magnesium	15	20
Zinc	25	30
Copper	6	6

*Contains less than 2% of the U.S. RDA of these nutrients.

INGREDIENTS: Wheat Bran with other parts of wheat; Raisins; Sugar; Salt; Malt Flavoring; Partially Hydrogenated Vegetable Oil (One or More of: Coconut, Soybean, and Palm); Invert Syrup; Vitamin A Palmitate; Reduced Iron; Zinc Oxide; Niacinamide; Pyridoxine Hydrochloride (B6); Thiamin Hydrochloride (B1); Riboflavin (B2); Folic Acid; Vitamin B12; and Vitamin D2.

CARBOHYDRATE INFORMATION

	Raisin Bran	
	1 oz. Cereal & 1/3 oz. raisins	with 1/2 cup whole milk
Starch and Related Carbohydrates	12 g	12 g
Sucrose and Other Sugars	13 g	19 g
Dietary Fiber	4 g	4 g
Total Carbohydrates	29 g	35 g

Values by Formulation and Analysis.

Summary

Tap Prior Knowledge

"Make a Summary": Ask the students how big the oceans are in relation to the continents' land size. Ask them how people can explore the bottom of the ocean.

"The Inuit": Ask the students what they know about the climate of the Arctic region. Would they like to live there? Do they know of any people who do live in the Arctic region?

"The Red Scare and McCarthyism": Ask the students if they have ever been accused of doing something they did not do. How did they feel? What did they do?

Skill to Emphasize

Review the section about summary on page 23. Tell the students that a summary leaves out unimportant ideas and details. A good summary is short and to the point. The title and subtitles in an article can help students to write a good summary.

Preview Text Features

Preview the article with students. Have the students pay attention to the title and details in the article. These details will help them arrive at a main idea and write a better summary. Point out the illustration. Boldfaced words indicate vocabulary words

Comprehending the Selection

Model how to summarize the article by asking: *What are the important ideas and details in this article?*

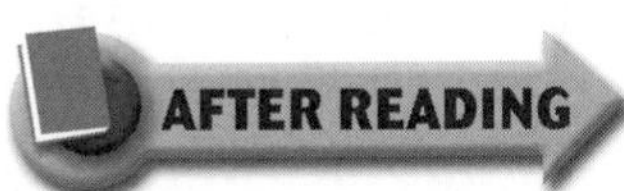

Reinforce the Comprehension Skill

Tell the students that a good summary is short, and it includes only the most important ideas in the article. Distribute copies of the Summary Chart on page 119. Have the students complete the chart for the articles to help them write their summaries.

Assess

Have the students complete the activities for the selection.

Have the students write about how they might feel if they were falsely accused of a crime. What would they do? How could they defend themselves against the false charges?

Have the students search through the newspaper or news magazines for articles about people who are somewhat removed from modern society, such as tribes deep in the Amazon or hermits. Have the students summarize the articles. Then have the students bring their articles and summaries to share with the class.

SELECTION DETAILS

Summary

"Make a Summary" (sample paragraph, page 40): The sample paragraph give practice in summarizing the main idea and details in a short selection about the oceans.

"The Inuit" (page 41): This article gives information about these Arctic people, including the changes in their lifestyle.

"The Red Scare and McCarthyism" (page 43): This article deals with the fear of Communism after World War II and the extreme measures used to combat Communism in the United States.

Selection Type

Social Studies Articles

Comprehension Skill

Summarize Information

Standards

Reading

- Summarize the main information in a nonfiction text.

Social Studies

- Explain ways that humans depend upon limited resources and adapt to, and affect, the natural environment.
- Analyze the Red Scare, including McCarthyism and the House Un-American Activities Committee.

VOCABULARY

Introduce the vocabulary words. Write the words on the board. Help students find a definition for each word. Have students use each word in a sentence.

"Make a Summary"
sonar *decompression*
procedures

"The Inuit"
soapstone *community*
traditional

"The Red Scare and McCarthyism"
communism *McCarthyism*
investigate

Name ______________________________ Date ____________

Make a Summary

A summary is a short account of the main idea and key details of an article. A summary should include only the most important points in an article. Summaries are good for condensing the information in an article. Remember, you can often find the main idea of a paragraph in the first or last sentence. Pay attention to the major ideas and details in this article.

The Oceans

The oceans cover about two thirds of the Earth's surface. The great majority of Earth's water is in the oceans, and most of this is salt water. The oceans can be several miles deep, but most of the life in the oceans exists in the top 200 meters of water.

Over nine tenths of the Earth's water is salty. Salt is a natural resource that is dissolved in ocean water. Salt water is not good for drinking. But objects do float more easily in salt water than in fresh water. Salt water also freezes more slowly than fresh water. This is one reason the oceans do not freeze in very cold climates.

The ocean floor is not a flat, wide plain. Instead, the ocean floor contains many of the same landform features found on the continents. The ocean floor does have plains, but it also has slopes, hills, mountains, valleys, and volcanoes. The oceans contain mid-ocean ridges, which are long chains of mountains that run along the ocean floor.

Measuring the depths of the oceans is not an easy task. Scientists use a method called **sonar**. Sound waves are aimed at the ocean floor. Based on their rate of travel, the sound waves can be timed. These times can then be used to calculate the depth of the ocean floor.

As the depth of the ocean water increases, its pressure also increases. As a result, deep-sea divers and explorers need to use special equipment and to observe certain **procedures** when they make their dives. One procedure is called **decompression**. In this procedure, divers must rise back to the surface slowly, or bubbles of nitrogen gas can occur in their blood, causing a painful condition called "the bends."

Write the major idea from each paragraph. Then, combine these ideas to write a summary in your own words. Write complete sentences. Use a separate piece of paper to write your summary.

Paragraph 1: ____

____

Paragraph 2: ____

____

Paragraph 3: ____

____

Paragraph 4: ____

____

Paragraph 5: ____

____

Name ______________________________ Date ______________

The Inuit

The Inuit people live throughout the Arctic regions. They live in parts of Canada, Greenland, Alaska, and even in Russia. Canada has about 30,000 Inuit. The word *Inuit* means "the people."

Many of Canada's Inuit live in the Northwest Territories near the Beaufort Sea. The climate in this region is very cold. Winter temperatures stay below freezing, and ice and snow cover the land for many months. Summers are short and chilly.

For centuries, the Inuit hunted whale, walrus, reindeer, and seal for food. Inuit homes were made from blocks of ice or animal skins. The Inuit used sleds to get from one place to another. The sleds were pulled by strong dogs with thick coats.

Today, life has changed for the Inuit people. Most of them no longer hunt for food. Instead, they buy food at a grocery store. New tools have also changed the way the Inuit people live. They use snowmobiles instead of dogsleds in many places. Airplanes carry people and supplies across the huge frozen areas of northern Canada.

Yet the traditional ways are important in many Inuit communities. Inuit artists still carve jewelry and stone sculptures from **soapstone**, a soft, smooth stone. Some Inuit have begun to use dogsleds again. Dogs do not run out of fuel or break down, as snowmobiles sometimes do. In the cold climate of northern Canada, this can sometimes mean the difference between life and death.

Today, many Inuit are fighting to keep their **traditional** ways of life from being forgotten. They are trying to make sure that their children will learn about the old ways from their parents and relatives in the **community**.

List the major ideas and details in this article.

____

____

____

____

____

____

____

____

____

____

Name ______________________________ Date______________

Comprehension Review

Darken the circle by the best answer.

1. The Inuit people live throughout the _____ regions.
   Ⓐ Antarctic
   Ⓑ Australian
   Ⓒ Arctic
   Ⓓ African

2. For centuries, the Inuit hunted whale, walrus, reindeer, and _____ for food.
   Ⓐ bear
   Ⓑ wolf
   Ⓒ elephants
   Ⓓ seal

3. This article is mainly about _____.
   Ⓐ how the Inuit carve soapstone
   Ⓑ how the Inuit people have changed over time
   Ⓒ dogsleds and airplanes
   Ⓓ how to hunt a walrus

4. From the article, you can conclude that _____.
   Ⓐ the Inuit people do not live in Alaska
   Ⓑ the climate in the Northwest Territories is tropical
   Ⓒ the dogs got tired of pulling the dogsleds
   Ⓓ some Inuit are trying to restore the old ways of life

5. A community is _____.
   Ⓐ a group of people living and working together
   Ⓑ a way to send messages
   Ⓒ a soft stone good for carving
   Ⓓ a kind of dogsled

6. The word *Inuit* means _____.
   Ⓐ whale hunter
   Ⓑ the peephole
   Ⓒ the people
   Ⓓ look over there

Use your list on page 41 to write a summary of the article. Write complete sentences. Use another piece of paper if necessary.

____

____

____

____

____

____

____

____

____

____

Name ________________________________ Date ______________

The Red Scare and McCarthyism

Senator Joseph McCarthy

The fear of **communism** was strong in the United States in the early 1920s and again after World War II. Because of the fear of communism, President Truman had the loyalty of three million federal workers checked. Freedom of speech and freedom of the press were in danger of being lost.

The House of Representatives formed the House Committee on Un-American Activities (HUAC) to find Communists in the government. In 1948 the Committee **investigated** Alger Hiss, an important person in the State Department. Hiss was accused of being a Communist spy. Hiss said he was innocent. The HUAC did not prove that Hiss was guilty of spying, but he was found guilty of lying during his trial.

Senator Joseph McCarthy spread the fear of communism to every part of the nation. In 1950 McCarthy made a speech in which he said he had the names of 205 Communists in the State Department. McCarthy never named the people on his list nor did he prove they were guilty. But he continued to accuse many Americans of being Communists, and he ruined many of their careers. Even Presidents Truman and Eisenhower were called traitors. Most senators and representatives were afraid to speak out against McCarthy. They feared that they, too, would be accused of being Communists. However, Senator Margaret Chase Smith and six other senators did have the courage to speak out against McCarthy. Edward R. Murrow made television shows that reported how McCarthy had falsely accused people.

In 1954 McCarthy lost his power after he attacked the army for being filled with Communists. The Senate took action and made a statement against McCarthy. The fear of communism remained strong through the 1980s. **McCarthyism** now means the policy of falsely accusing people of working against the government.

List the major ideas and details in this article.

____

____

____

____

____

____

____

____

Name ______________________________ Date ______________

Comprehension and Vocabulary Review

Darken the circle by the best answer.

1. Joseph McCarthy was a _____.
   Ⓐ President
   Ⓑ Representative
   Ⓒ Communist
   Ⓓ Senator

2. McCarthy lost his power in 1954 after he _____.
   Ⓐ got tired of looking for Communists
   Ⓑ attacked the army for being filled with Communists
   Ⓒ was elected Vice President
   Ⓓ proved that Alger Hiss was guilty

3. Alger Hiss was an important person in _____.
   Ⓐ Russia
   Ⓑ the House of Representatives
   Ⓒ the Senate
   Ⓓ the State Department

4. You can conclude from the article that _____.
   Ⓐ Alger Hiss was found guilty of being a spy
   Ⓑ Joseph McCarthy did not like Communists
   Ⓒ President Eisenhower was a Communist
   Ⓓ Joseph McCarthy always told the truth

5. _____ made TV shows about how McCarthy falsely accused people.
   Ⓐ Edward R. Murrow
   Ⓑ Alger Hiss
   Ⓒ Margaret Chase Smith
   Ⓓ HUAC

6. *McCarthyism* now means _____.
   Ⓐ listening to the music of the Beatles
   Ⓑ being a Communist
   Ⓒ falsely accusing people of being against the government
   Ⓓ losing the freedom of speech

Use your list on page 43 to write a summary of the article. Write complete sentences. Use another piece of paper if necessary.

UNIT 3 Narration

Narration is concerned with the sequence of events or details in time. Sometimes this sequence is presented as a plot, as in a short story or historical narrative. Sometimes the sequence is a list, as in a how-to project. The sequence usually goes from beginning to end in chronological order, just as we move through time. Many times, a strong relationship exists between events. One event may cause another event. This relationship is called cause and effect.

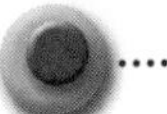

Sequence

Sequence is the order of events in a narrative or process. Students should be able to retell the order of events in a narration. Some words serve as signals to show the order of events. Such words are *first, next, then*, and *finally*. Lists may also be used in a selection to show order. Often, these lists are arranged alphabetically or numerically.

To find the sequence of an event or process:
- Use the Sequence Chart on page 120.
- Read the article carefully.
- Look for signal words or numbers that show the order of events.
- Think about the sequence, or order of events.
- Decide in what order events occurred.
- Retell or write a brief list of the events in order.

Narration of Event (Lesson 8)

Narration of event is a form that should be familiar to students. They often tell stories of what they did. They read stories of fictional characters. Both of these kinds of stories contain narration of events. So do biographies and historical occurrences. A biography tells the events in a person's life. A historical occurrence also contains a narration of events, such as the sequence of events in World War II.

A narration of event usually includes a sense of beginning, middle, and end. It should have a setting and at least one person or historical character. A problem is usually introduced, and some outcome to the problem is indicated. The narration of event may include some emotional impact and may include an insight or point about human nature or behavior.

To recall the sequence in a narration of event:
- Use the Sequence Chart on page 120.
- Read the title for information about the event or person.
- Read the article carefully.
- Look for signal words that show the order of events.
- Decide in what order the events occurred.
- Divide the event into beginning, middle, and end.
- Retell or write a brief list of the events in order.

Narration of Process (Lesson 9)

Narration of process is another form that should be familiar to students. One kind of process is the how-to. A how-to can be instructional, such as how to bake a cake, or it can be informational, such as how glass is made. Some processes can be quite complicated, such as the annual migratory cycle of some animals.

A narration of process includes a series of steps that also presents a sense of beginning, middle, and end. The end should indicate the completion of the process. The process essay may also include a list of materials needed, a cautionary list of things to do and not to do, and any tips or shortcuts that will facilitate the process.

To recall the sequence in a narration of process:
- Use the Sequence Chart on page 120.
- Read the title for information about the process.
- Read the article carefully.
- Look for signal words or numbers that show the order of steps.
- Note what the end result should be.
- Retell or write a brief list of the steps in order.

Cause and Effect (Lesson 10)

An article can tell about things that happen and why they happen. Why something happens is a cause. What happens because of it is an effect. In other words, a cause tells why an effect happens. Some words are used to signal causes and effects. The words *because* and *since* often introduce a cause. The words *therefore, so, thus*, and *as a result* often introduce an effect.

To identify causes and effects:
- Use the Cause-Effect Chart on page 121.
- Read the title for information about a cause or effect.
- Read the article carefully.
- Look for signal words that introduce a cause or effect.
- Decide which part of a sentence or paragraph is the cause and which part is the effect.
- Use that information to help answer *Why?*

Graphic Organizers

Sequence Chart	page 120
Cause-Effect Chart	page 121

Narration of Event

Tap Prior Knowledge

"Everett Alvarez, Jr.": Ask the students if they know what a prisoner of war is. How do they think such prisoners are treated by the enemy?

"The Calendar We Use": Ask the students who they think developed the calendar they use. What do they think calendars are supposed to do?

"Jesse Owens (1913–1980)": Ask the students if they have ever watched the Summer Olympics. Ask them if they have heard about Adolph Hitler or Jesse Owens. What do they know about these men?

"To the Top of Annapurna": Ask the students if they would like to climb a tall mountain. How would they feel about climbing in freezing temperatures with the constant threat of avalanches?

Skill to Emphasize

Review the section about narration of event on page 45. Tell the students that they will try to find the sequence, or order, of events in each article. An event is something that happens. A narration tells about a series of events. The events occur in a certain order, called a sequence.

Preview Text Features

Point out the title of each article. The titles give the students information about the important events they will read about. The title in the Owens article also includes the span of years of his life. Point out the words, times, or dates that suggest the sequence in the articles. Boldfaced words indicate vocabulary words.

Point out the dialogue in the Annapurna article. These words spoken by a person in the event give information and emotions about the event. However, many times such dialogue is fictional. Writers make up what they think someone in history might have said. Students should be able to distinguish what is fictional against a factual background. Many times the words of famous people are recorded. Other times, though, writers simply dramatize a scene from history, and the dialogue is fictional. Because Arlene Blum used a tape recorder, the words in this article are more likely factual.

Comprehending the Selection

Model how to identify the sequence by asking: *What words or clues tell you the order of events?*

Reinforce the Comprehension Skill

Tell the students that in most narrations of event, the sequence will be in chronological order. This means the events are presented in the article just as they happen in time. The events can be presented by the hour, day, month, or year.

Distribute copies of the Sequence Chart on page 120. Have the students complete the chart for the articles. They can use another sheet of paper if necessary.

Assess

Have the students complete the activities for the selection.

SELECTION DETAILS

Summary

"Everett Alvarez, Jr." (page 47): The article tells about an American pilot who was shot down over North Vietnam and served as a prisoner of war longer than any other American.

"The Calendar We Use" (page 48): This article tells of the development of the modern calendar.

"Jesse Owens (1913–1980)" (page 49): This article tells about the life of Jesse Owens and his performance in the 1936 Olympics.

"To the Top of Annapurna" (page 51): The article tells about a group of women who struggled to climb a mountain in Nepal.

Selection Type

Social Studies Articles

Comprehension Skill

Identify Sequence of Events in a Narration of Event

Standards

Reading

- Identify the order of events in a reading selection.

History

- Put in chronological order important people and events.
- Describe how ancient civilizations have had an effect on later civilizations.

VOCABULARY

"Everett Alvarez, Jr."
prisoner of war, criticize, tortured, cease-fire

"The Calendar We Use"
compatible, *recurring, uncooperative, Gregorian calendar, Julian calendar, sophisticated*

"Jesse Owens (1913–1980)"
sharecropper, dictator, inferior, superior

"To the Top of Annapurna"
summit, accompany, perished

Name ______________________________ Date______________

Everett Alvarez, Jr.

Everett Alvarez, Jr., on the left

Everett Alvarez, Jr., was the first American pilot shot down while flying over North Vietnam. He spent more time as a **prisoner of war** than any other American.

Alvarez was born in California to a Mexican American family. He became the first person in his family to graduate from college. After college he joined the Navy. He became a fighter pilot and was sent to Vietnam. In August 1964, Alvarez's plane was shot down over North Vietnam. He was captured and he became a prisoner of war, or POW.

For more than eight years, Alvarez suffered terribly in a filthy North Vietnamese prison. He was beaten and **tortured**. He was given very little to eat, and the food that he was given was often full of bugs. Alvarez's hardest time in prison was when he learned that his wife had divorced him and had married another man. The North Vietnamese wanted Alvarez to **criticize** the United States publicly. However, the loyal pilot refused to speak out against America, even when he was tortured.

After the **cease-fire** in 1973, Alvarez was returned to the United States. Upon landing, he spoke on television to the nation: "For years and years we dreamed of this day and we kept the faith. . . . We have come home. God bless the President and God bless you Mr. and Mrs. America. You did not forget us."

Alvarez rebuilt his life. He became a lawyer, married again, and had two sons. After the Vietnam Veterans Memorial was completed, Alvarez spoke at its dedication ceremony in Washington, D.C. In California, there is a high school named for Everett Alvarez. From Alvarez's story, students learn the importance of hard work, a good education, and loyalty to the United States.

Darken the circle by the best answer.

1. Everett Alvarez, Jr., was a prisoner of war in _____.
   - Ⓐ California
   - Ⓑ the United States
   - Ⓒ North Vietnam
   - Ⓓ Mexico

2. After Alvarez became a fighter pilot, _____.
   - Ⓐ he graduated from college
   - Ⓑ he joined the Navy
   - Ⓒ he joined the Army
   - Ⓓ he was sent to Vietnam

3. After Alvarez became a prisoner of war, _____.
   - Ⓐ he divorced his wife
   - Ⓑ he was tortured and beaten
   - Ⓒ he was given plenty to eat
   - Ⓓ he became a fighter pilot

4. After the cease-fire in 1973, _____
   - Ⓐ Alvarez's plane was shot down
   - Ⓑ Alvarez's wife divorced him
   - Ⓒ he was returned to the United States
   - Ⓓ he was put in a North Vietnamese prison

Name ______________________________ Date ____________

The Calendar We Use

Julius Caesar

For hundreds of years, calendar makers struggled with the problem of how to develop a calendar that would be **compatible** with the regular, natural rhythms of the Sun, Moon, and the stars. There are about $29\frac{1}{2}$ days between each New Moon, and about $365\frac{1}{4}$ days in a year, marked by the annual cycle of the seasons. This means that there are more than 12—but fewer than 13—lunar months in a year.

Centuries passed as various cultures devised systems that would work with those **uncooperative** heavenly cycles. When they finally came up with a workable calendar, it became even more important than the natural rhythms on which it was modeled.

Before Julius Caesar's **Julian calendar**, people thought of time as a **recurring** cycle of natural events. They didn't think much about ideas of *past* and *future*. When the Julian calendar came into being nearly sixteen centuries before the **Gregorian calendar**, other ways of marking time were developed, such as **sophisticated** sundials and water clocks. People were able to plan their lives without having to depend on the Moon, the seasons, and their gods.

When our modern calendar finally came into being, it happened in the city of Rome, where Caesar once ruled. The calendar that nearly all the world uses today was established by Pope Gregory XLII and his advisors during the 1570s. The Gregorian calendar is based on an average year of 365 days, five hours, 48 minutes and 20 seconds, which is just 26 seconds off the true value. This will build up to an error of one full day by the year 4909. Maybe someone will think of a way to correct that.

Darken the circle by the best answer for each question.

1. Which calendar came first?
   Ⓐ the Gregorian calendar
   Ⓑ seasonal calendars
   Ⓒ the Julian calendar
   Ⓓ Cal's calendar

2. Which would be another good title for this selection?
   Ⓐ Julius Caesar's Calendar
   Ⓑ The Search for a Perfect Calendar
   Ⓒ The Moon, the Sun, and the Seasons
   Ⓓ Sophisticated Sundials and Water Clocks

3. What does the word *compatible* mean in this selection?
   Ⓐ in agreement
   Ⓑ inappropriate
   Ⓒ friendly
   Ⓓ unusual

4. Using the Gregorian calendar, how long will pass before an error of one full day takes place?
   Ⓐ less than 3,000 years
   Ⓑ less than 1,000 years
   Ⓒ more than 3,000 years
   Ⓓ more than 5,000 years

Name ______________________________ Date ______________

Jesse Owens (1913–1980)

Jesse Owens

Jesse Owens won four gold medals at the 1936 Olympic Games. This great athlete was born in Alabama to a poor family with nine children. His grandfather had been a slave. Owens's father was a **sharecropper** who struggled to earn enough money for his family.

In 1921, Owens's family moved to Ohio. When Owens was in the fifth grade, the coach at his school asked him to join the track team. After six years of training, Owens became a high-school track star. After high school, Owens studied at Ohio State University. Owens attended classes, trained for the track team, and worked at three part-time jobs.

At a track meet in 1935, Owens broke four track records for running and jumping. He was chosen to represent the United States in the 1936 Olympic Games. The Olympics were to be held in Berlin, Germany.

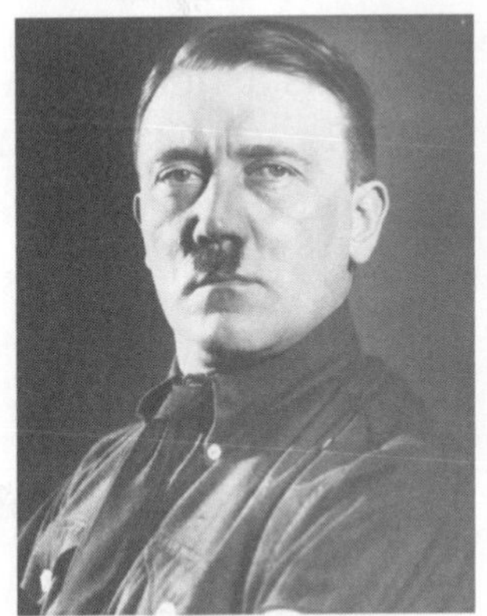

Adolf Hitler

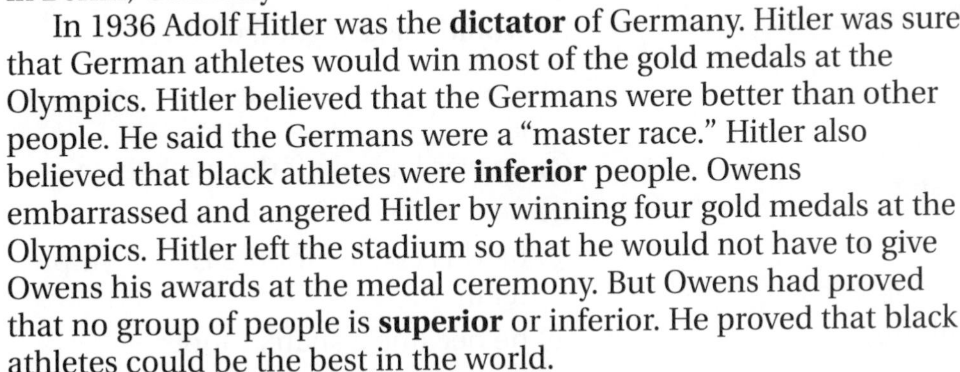

In 1936 Adolf Hitler was the **dictator** of Germany. Hitler was sure that German athletes would win most of the gold medals at the Olympics. Hitler believed that the Germans were better than other people. He said the Germans were a "master race." Hitler also believed that black athletes were **inferior** people. Owens embarrassed and angered Hitler by winning four gold medals at the Olympics. Hitler left the stadium so that he would not have to give Owens his awards at the medal ceremony. But Owens had proved that no group of people is **superior** or inferior. He proved that black athletes could be the best in the world.

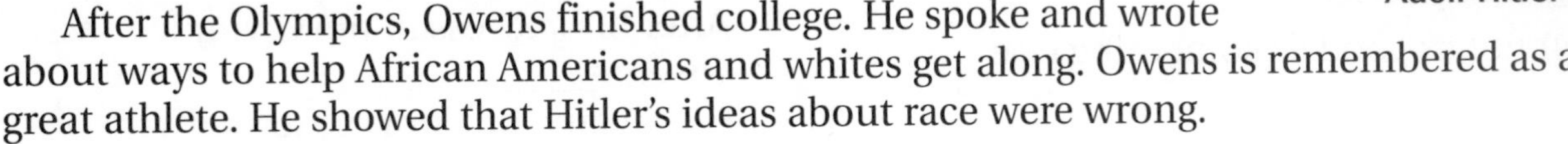

After the Olympics, Owens finished college. He spoke and wrote about ways to help African Americans and whites get along. Owens is remembered as a great athlete. He showed that Hitler's ideas about race were wrong.

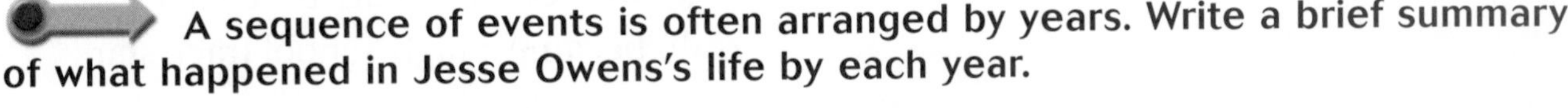

A sequence of events is often arranged by years. Write a brief summary of what happened in Jesse Owens's life by each year.

1913 ____

1921 ____

1935 ____

____

1936 ____

____

1980 ____

Name ________________________________ Date______________

Comprehension and Vocabulary Review

Darken the circle by the best answer.

1. In 1936, _____ was the dictator of Germany.
   Ⓐ Jesse Owens
   Ⓑ O. Lympics
   Ⓒ Adolf Hitler
   Ⓓ Master Race

2. Jesse Owens was born in _____.
   Ⓐ Ohio
   Ⓑ Germany
   Ⓒ Berlin
   Ⓓ Alabama

3. This article is mainly about _____.
   Ⓐ the 1936 Olympics
   Ⓑ the life of Jesse Owens
   Ⓒ Adolf Hitler as dictator
   Ⓓ how to be a track star

4. *Inferior* means _____.
   Ⓐ better than something else
   Ⓑ the inside of a building
   Ⓒ always frightened
   Ⓓ not as good as something else

5. You can conclude that Adolf Hitler _____.
   Ⓐ did not want Jesse Owens to win
   Ⓑ could not run very fast
   Ⓒ wanted to keep Owen's medals for himself
   Ⓓ thought Jesse Owens was a superior athlete

6. You can infer that a sharecropper _____.
   Ⓐ is a track coach
   Ⓑ gets a share of the crops he grows
   Ⓒ speaks German well
   Ⓓ would make a good dictator

7. After Jesse Owens broke four records in 1935, _____.
   Ⓐ he was kicked off the track team
   Ⓑ he was tested for steroids
   Ⓒ he was chosen for the U.S. Olympic team
   Ⓓ he became a sharecropper

8. After his success in the Olympics, Jesse Owens _____.
   Ⓐ became dictator of Germany
   Ⓑ finished college
   Ⓒ worked three part-time jobs
   Ⓓ became a high-school track star

Write About It.

Adolf Hitler thought black athletes were inferior. How do you think Hitler felt as he watched Jesse Owens win four gold medals? Write a few complete sentences to tell how Hitler might have felt. Use another piece of paper if necessary.

____

____

____

____

Name ______________________________ Date______________

To the Top of Annapurna

Arlene Blum spoke softly into her tape recorder. "There were so many **avalanches** yesterday," she said. "It gives you a scary feeling. I keep wondering when the next avalanche will come."

Blum stopped for a moment. She glanced up at the snow-covered mountain named Annapurna. Would the snow come rushing down again today? If it did, would it sweep her and the others away? Blum felt fear in the pit of her stomach. She spoke into the tape recorder once more. "Maybe we shouldn't climb today," she said.

Blum and her crew did end up climbing on that day. After all, that was why they had come to this 26,504-foot mountain in Nepal, a country north of India. They wanted to climb Annapurna. It was the tenth highest mountain in the world. Few people had ever reached its **summit**; seven had **perished** trying.

Arlene Blum's team was the first of its kind. Its members were all women. No all-woman group had ever climbed a mountain this high. Blum's group used Sherpa guides who were men, just as other climbing teams did, but everyone else was a woman.

The women began climbing on August 28, 1978. They soon hit ice walls 500 feet high. The threat of a deadly avalanche always hung over them. They ran into wild storms. During one blizzard, their Sherpa guides quit, but Blum promised them more money, and they agreed to come back. Finally, on October 13, the team reached the 24,200-foot mark, where they set up a camp. Two days later, they would make the final push for the top.

Blum picked two small groups to climb to the summit. The rest would stay at the camp. For the first group Blum chose Piro Kramer, Irene Miller, and Vera Komarkova. She picked two Sherpa guides to **accompany** them.

The group woke up at 3 A.M. on October 15. It was about ten degrees below zero. That far up, there was not much oxygen in the air. Everyone had to move slowly. While she was getting ready, Kramer took off her gloves. The tip of one finger was frozen. She knew right away that she would not go to the top. She said, "I'd rather lose the summit than my finger."

At 7 A.M. the others began the final climb. The snow was sometimes up to their knees. They had to breathe six times just to take one step. Often they wondered if they could keep going, but none of them quit. They just kept climbing. At last, at 3:30 P.M., all four reached the top. The women stuck an American flag into the snow. Then they hugged each other. They had made it!

Arlene Blum at the foot of Annapurna

Name ______________________________ Date ____________

A second team tried to reach the summit two days later. Their guide soon got sick. He returned to the camp. But Vera Watson and Alison Chadwick kept going. That night Blum tried to contact the two women by radio, but she got no answer. In the morning she scanned the mountain. She could not see Watson or Chadwick, and fear grew with each passing minute. What had happened to them?

Two days later that question was answered. Guides had been sent to look for the two women. They spotted the bodies of Watson and Chadwick lying at the bottom of a 1,500-foot cliff. One of them had probably slipped on the ice. Since they were roped together, they had both fallen to their death. The team's joy instantly turned to sadness.

Carefully the team went back down the mountain. They had completed the toughest climb of their lives. They had conquered Annapurna. But they had also lost two dear friends. For Blum and the others, Annapurna would always be a symbol of both victory and loss.

Sequence Review

The sequence of events is the order in which the events occur. Often, times or dates are used to heip you understand the sequence. In this article, dates and times are used to tell when each event occurred.

Reread the article. Then write complete sentences to describe the event that occurred at each date or time.

August 28, 1978 ______________________________

____

October 13, 1978 ______________________________

____

October 15, 1978 ______________________________

3:00 A.M. ______________________________

7:00 A.M. ______________________________

____

3:30 P.M. ______________________________

____

October 17, 1978 ______________________________

____

October 19, 1978 ______________________________

____

Name ______________________________ Date ____________

Comprehension and Vocabulary Review

Darken the circle by the best answer.

1. Annapurna is a mountain in _____.
   Ⓐ the United States
   Ⓑ India
   Ⓒ Nepal
   Ⓓ Sherpa

2. After the women began climbing on August 28, _____.
   Ⓐ an avalanche covered them all
   Ⓑ they soon hit very tall ice walls
   Ⓒ they reached the summit that afternoon
   Ⓓ they decided to stop climbing

3. This article is mainly about _____.
   Ⓐ how Sherpa guides don't like to work
   Ⓑ how avalanches can be dangerous
   Ⓒ how mountain climbers should have a tape recorder
   Ⓓ a group of women who climbed a tall mountain

4. An avalanche is _____.
   Ⓐ a wild animal
   Ⓑ an unfriendly climber
   Ⓒ a snow slide
   Ⓓ a kind of storm

5. You can conclude that the women _____.
   Ⓐ did not know how to climb mountains
   Ⓑ were happy and sad about their adventure
   Ⓒ did not care about their fingers
   Ⓓ should have had more men to help them

6. The summit is _____.
   Ⓐ the highest part of the mountain
   Ⓑ the lowest part of the mountain
   Ⓒ a dangerous avalanche
   Ⓓ a wild blizzard

7. Seven people had perished trying to climb Annapurna. *Perished* means _____.
   Ⓐ started
   Ⓑ died
   Ⓒ fallen
   Ⓓ succeeded

8. The last thing the women did was _____.
   Ⓐ to climb to the summit
   Ⓑ to set up their base camp
   Ⓒ to find the two dead women
   Ⓓ to go back down the mountain

Write complete sentences to answer the question. Use another piece of paper if necessary.

9. Writers sometimes make up what they think someone in history might have said. Students should be able to distinguish what is fictional against a factual background. Many times the words of famous people are recorded. Other times, though, writers simply dramatize a scene from history, and the dialogue is fictional. There are words that Arlene Blum said at the beginning of the article. Do you really think she said those words? Why or why not?

Narration of Process

SELECTION DETAILS

Summary

"Find Your Weight on Other Planets" (page 55): This article shows students how to figure their weight on another planet based on gravitational pull.

"Niagara Falls" (page 56): This article tells how Niagara Falls was formed and how its waters are used to generate electric power.

"Life Cycle of a Star" (page 57): This article is an informational narration of process that tells about how a star is born and dies.

Selection Type

Mathematics Article
Science Articles

Comprehension Skill

Identify Sequence of Events in a Narration of Process

Standards

Reading

- Identify the order of steps in a reading selection.
- Use features of a reading selection such as lists and charts.

Mathematics

- Compute using whole numbers and decimals.

Science

- Explain how Earth processes seen today, including erosion, are similar to those that occurred in the past.
- Describe common objects in the solar system, galaxy, and universe.

VOCABULARY

"Find Your Weight on Other Planets"
gravitational

"Niagara Falls"
gigantic, retreating, escarpment, turbines

"Life Cycle of a Star"
nebula, white dwarf, protostar, supernova, nuclear, neutron star, red giant, black hole

Tap Prior Knowledge

"Find Your Weight on Other Planets": Ask the students if they have ever seen movies of the astronauts bouncing around on the Moon. How much do they think they would weigh on the Moon or the other planets?

"Niagara Falls": Ask the students if they have ever seen pictures of Niagara Falls or some other waterfall. How are waterfalls formed?

"Life Cycle of a Star": Do the students know that the Sun is a star? What will happen to the Sun when it runs out of fuel?

Skill to Emphasize

Review the section about narration of process on page 45. Tell the students that they will try to find the sequence, or order, of steps in each article. A process is a way in which something is done, such as how to bake a cake or how a star develops.

Preview Text Features

Point out the titles of the articles. The titles give the students information about the process they will read about. Point out the chart in "Find Your Weight on Other Planets." Boldfaced words in the articles indicate vocabulary words.

Comprehending the Selection

Model how to identify the sequence by asking: *What words or clues tell you the order of steps in the process?*

Reinforce the Comprehension Skill

Tell the students that in a narration of process, the sequence will be in chronological order. The steps in a how-to are presented in the order they should be done.

Distribute copies of the Sequence Chart on page 120. Have the students complete the chart for "Niagara Falls" and "Life Cycle of a Star." They can use another sheet of paper if necessary.

Assess

Have the students complete the activities for the selection.

Have the students write a how-to process about something they know how to do well.

Name ______________________________ Date ______________

Find Your Weight on Other Planets

The planets are different sizes. Some are larger than Earth, and some are smaller. The **gravitational** pulls of the planets are different, too. If you could go to the planets, you would have a different weight on each one. On Mars, for example, the gravitational pull is 38 percent of that on Earth. So, on Mars your weight would be about one third your Earth weight.

To find out exactly how weight changes, try this. Suppose you weigh 50 kilograms, or about 110 pounds. What would you weigh on Mars?

1. Mars has a surface gravity of 38%.
2. Change 38% to 0.38.
3. Multiply 50 kilograms x 0.38 = 19 kilograms, or about 42 pounds.
4. Complete the chart below.

Planet	Surface gravity compared with Earth	Weight of person who weighs 50 kilograms on Earth
Mercury	28%	
Venus	85%	
Mars	38%	19 kg
Jupiter	260%	
Saturn	120%	
Uranus	110%	
Neptune	140%	

The surface gravity of Pluto is not known.

Use the chart to answer each question.

1. On which planet would you probably weigh the least? ______________
2. On which planet would you weigh the most? ______________
3. On which planets would you weigh more than you weigh on Earth?

____

4. On which planets would you weigh less than you weigh on Earth?

____

5. On Venus, the apples are the ripest in the solar system. You need 5 pounds (Earth weight). How much should you have the clerk weigh out for you? ______________
6. If you also pick up 10 pounds of pickles and 7 pounds of cole slaw on Venus, how much cole slaw and pickles will you have when you arrive on Mercury? ______________

Name ______________________________ Date ____________

Niagara Falls

Niagara Falls is one of nature's greatest wonders. Its **gigantic** waterfalls were formed when the last glaciers were **retreating** north. The melting glaciers formed five giant fresh-water lakes, now called the Great Lakes. One of these lakes, Lake Erie, ran downhill toward another, Lake Ontario. The water rushing from Lake Erie to Lake Ontario carved out the Niagara River. At one point the water passed over a steep cliff called the Niagara **Escarpment**, creating the falls. Since the original falls were formed over 10,000 years ago, the water has worn away the land back up the river. Each year the falls move from one to five feet closer to Lake Erie.

Yet Niagara Falls is more than a great tourist attraction. It provides electric power for thousands of homes. In 1950, both the United States and Canada, the two countries bordering the falls, agreed to develop ways to harness this water power.

First, water was diverted from the river flowing into the falls into large underground pipes. The water traveled overland to below the lower rapids of the falls. Here, it was returned to the river and passed through **turbines**. These turbines power 13 generators of the Robert Moses Niagara Power Plant. This plant, opened in 1961, is one of the largest power stations in the world. The electricity generated by the plant is used in homes and businesses throughout the region.

Darken the circle by the best answer.

1. Niagara Falls is bordered by the United States and _____.
   - Ⓐ California
   - Ⓑ Canada
   - Ⓒ China
   - Ⓓ Cuba

2. Water from Lake Erie flows over the falls into _____.
   - Ⓐ the Gulf of Mexico
   - Ⓑ the Atlantic Ocean
   - Ⓒ Lake Michigan
   - Ⓓ Lake Ontario

Write complete sentences to answer each question. Include the important steps in the process.

3. How was Niagara Falls formed? ______________________________

____

____

4. How is the water power converted into electricity? ______________________________

____

____

____

____

Name ______________________________ Date ______________

Life Cycle of a Star

Like living things, stars are born, live, and die. Most stars begin life in a **nebula**, a collection of gas and dust in space. Inside the nebula, a cloud of hydrogen gas and dust, or **protostar**, forms. The cloud shrinks as gravity, a force that pulls objects together, draws the dust particles and hydrogen closer.

As the protostar becomes denser, or packed more tightly, the hydrogen particles move faster. They strike each other with great force. This motion makes the core grow hotter. Pressure builds, pushing back against the force of gravity. Temperatures inside the protostar increase. When a certain temperature is reached, **nuclear** reactions begin. The nuclear reactions produce energy that heats the gases around the protostar. The gases glow, beginning the life of a star.

Stars contain so much energy that the nuclear reactions inside can happen for millions, and even billions, of years. In time, however, more and more hydrogen changes into helium. The center of the star begins to shrink again. As the helium and other material in the core are squeezed together, temperatures increase. Outer layers of gas grow larger and cooler. They change color to form a **red giant**. If the star is large enough, the outer layer of gases may blow away. This leaves a much smaller **white dwarf**. A white dwarf is dense and hot. At the end of its life, it cools to become about the size of a planet.

The death of a very large star is much different. The core becomes so hot and dense that the outer layers explode. A **supernova** forms. Gases fly into space. After its death, the amount of material that remains after the explosion determines whether the star will be a **neutron star** or a **black hole**.

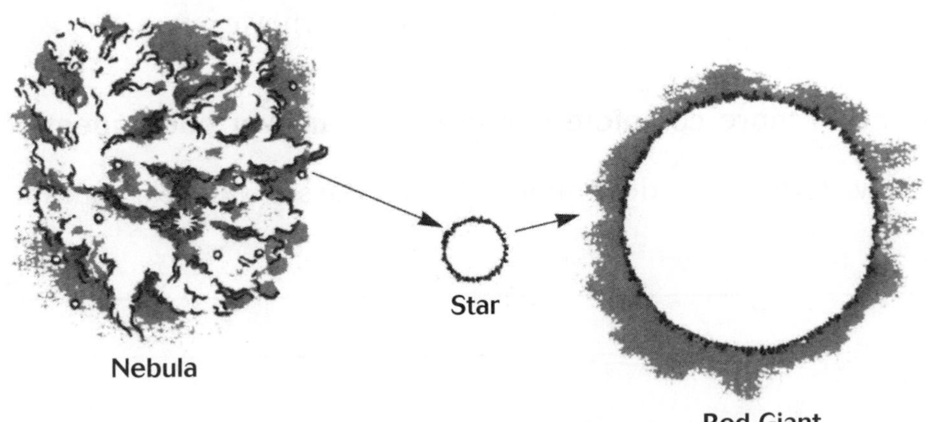

The stages in the life cycle of a star are given below. Write *1*, *2*, *3*, *4*, and *5* to show the correct order. The first one is done for you.

_____ red giant _____ white dwarf _____ protostar __1__ nebula _____ star

Name ______________________________ Date ____________

Comprehension and Vocabulary Review

Directions: Darken the circle by the best answer.

1. A collection of gas and dust floating in space is called a _____.
   Ⓐ fibula
   Ⓑ nebula
   Ⓒ supernova
   Ⓓ red giant

2. A cloud of _____ gas and dust can form a protostar.
   Ⓐ gravity
   Ⓑ helium
   Ⓒ hydrogen
   Ⓓ nebula

3. When a certain temperature is reached inside a protostar, _____.
   Ⓐ the protostar freezes
   Ⓑ the protostar explodes
   Ⓒ a supernova forms
   Ⓓ nuclear reactions begin

4. A large older star whose outer layers of gas cool is called a _____.
   Ⓐ protostar
   Ⓑ red giant
   Ⓒ nebula
   Ⓓ supernova

5. A _____ is a hot, dense star about the size of a planet.
   Ⓐ white dwarf
   Ⓑ red giant
   Ⓒ blue meanie
   Ⓓ neutron star

6. When a very large star dies, its outer gases explode into space and a _____ forms.
   Ⓐ protostar
   Ⓑ red giant
   Ⓒ nebula
   Ⓓ supernova

Write one or more complete sentences to answer each question.

7. After a supernova forms, what determines whether the star will be a neutron star or a black hole?

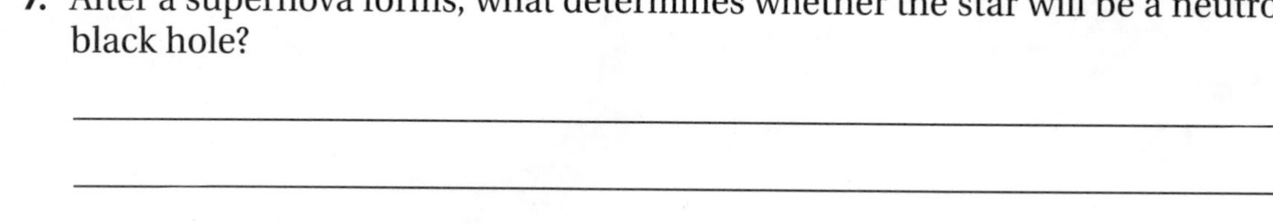

8. At what stage do you think the Sun is in its life cycle? Explain.

Cause and Effect

SELECTION DETAILS

Summary

"Find the Cause or Effect" (page 60): The sample paragraphs give practice in identifying causes and effects in short selections.

"The Dust Bowl" (page 62): This article tells the causes and effects of the Dust Bowl region in the 1930s.

"The Declaration of Independence" (page 63): This historical document gives the causes behind the American struggle for independence in the 1770s.

Selection Type

Social Studies Articles

Comprehension Skill

Identify Cause and Effect

Standards

Reading

- Understand cause and effect in a factual article.

Social Studies

- Identify major features of natural processes and forces that shape the Earth's surface.
- Learn the basic ideas set forth in the Declaration of Independence, Constitution, and Bill of Rights.

VOCABULARY

Introduce the vocabulary words for each article. Write the words on the board. Help students find a definition for each word. Have students use each word in a sentence.

"The Dust Bowl"

drought, disaster, conserve

"The Declaration of Independence"

adopted, sovereign, entitle, impel, endowed, unalienable, deriving, prudence, transient, usurpations, evinces, inestimable, formidable, tenure, render, invested, abdicated, mercenaries, insurrections, redress, unwarrantable, consanguinity, despotism, acquiesce, constrains, rectitude, assent, absolved, relinquish

Tap Prior Knowledge

"The Dust Bowl": Ask the students what they would do if the conditions where they live became so bad they could no longer live there. Do they know about the Dust Bowl of the 1930s and the journey of the Dust Bowl inhabitants to California? Have they read Steinbeck's *The Grapes of Wrath*?

"The Declaration of Independence": Ask the students if they know what is in the Declaration of Independence. Why is this document important in American history?

Skill to Emphasize

Review the section about cause and effect on page 45. Tell the students that many things that happen are caused by other things. What happens is an effect. What caused it to happen is a cause. Sometimes an effect then becomes a cause.

Preview Text Features

Point out the map in "The Dust Bowl" article. It shows the location of the Dust Bowl region. Point out the original Declaration of Independence and the paraphrase in the column beside it. Which of the two is easier to understand? Have the students look out for signal words that indicate a cause-effect relationship. Boldfaced words in the articles indicate vocabulary words.

Comprehending the Selection

Model how to identify causes and effects by asking: *What is one thing that happened in the article? What caused that thing to happen?*

Reinforce the Comprehension Skill

Tell the students that in cause-effect relationships, one cause can have many effects, and one effect can have many causes. Students should think about why things happen, then be able to identify the cause of events or the effects of causes.

Distribute copies of the Cause-Effect Chart on page 121. Have the students complete the chart for the articles.

Assess

Have the students complete the activities for the selection.

Have the students write about something that happened to them recently. Have them identify the causes of what happened.

Name ______________________________ Date ____________

Find the Cause or Effect

Read each paragraph. Darken the circle by the best answer for each question.

Henry Ford introduced the Model T in 1908. The design remained the same for many years. In 1913, Ford started making the Model T in a factory using an assembly line. Making lots of cars exactly the same brought down the cost of manufacturing them. By 1925, the price was down from $850 to just $260. At that price, people didn't have to be rich to buy a car.

1. What was the cause of the lower-priced cars?
Ⓐ the Model T
Ⓑ assembly line production
Ⓒ rich people
Ⓓ the same design

2. What was the effect of the lower prices?
Ⓐ Designs could change.
Ⓑ Factories were started.
Ⓒ More people could buy cars.
Ⓓ The price went down to $260.

Before the War of 1812, British ships often stopped and searched American ships. They were looking for English soldiers who had left England without permission. This action made Americans angry. President Thomas Jefferson requested that Congress declare an embargo. This meant that American ships could not leave American ports, nor could any foreign ships enter our ports. The idea was to keep England and France from getting badly needed American goods. When it became obvious that Americans were getting hurt by the embargo, Jefferson lifted it.

3. What was the cause of the embargo?
Ⓐ The British needed American goods.
Ⓑ The British searched American ships.
Ⓒ English soldiers left England without permission.
Ⓓ Jefferson lifted the embargo.

4. What was one effect of the embargo?
Ⓐ England and France needed American goods.
Ⓑ English soldiers left England.
Ⓒ American ships couldn't leave American ports.
Ⓓ The War of 1812 ended.

Name ______________________________ Date ____________

Read each paragraph. Darken the circle by the best answer for each question.

Most of the country of Norway is very close to the ocean. Therefore, fishing is an important industry. Fleets of ships leave from different port cities each day. These ships do not use rods to catch the great variety of marine life found in Norway's waters. They use nets. First, the sailors lay out their nets. They mark each location and then go on to lay others. When they return and lift their nets into the boats, they find many kinds of fish in the nets.

5. What is the effect of Norway's location near the ocean?
   - Ⓐ There are lots of beaches.
   - Ⓑ Fishing is a major industry.
   - Ⓒ Many sailors use nets.
   - Ⓓ Sailors lay out nets.

6. What is the cause of Norway's fishing industry?
   - Ⓐ They don't use rods to catch fish.
   - Ⓑ Ships leave port cities.
   - Ⓒ Norway is close to the ocean.
   - Ⓓ Many fish are caught in the nets.

Sometimes people aren't able to watch their favorite TV programs because they aren't on at a convenient time. Modern technology has made it easy for people to watch their favorite programs no matter what time they are on TV. With VCRs, people can tape a program and watch it at another time.

7. What is the cause of people using VCRs?
   - Ⓐ Programs aren't very good.
   - Ⓑ Modern technology is convenient.
   - Ⓒ TV programs don't come on at convenient times.
   - Ⓓ They can't watch TV programs.

8. What is the effect of having a VCR?
   - Ⓐ Modern tecnology makes things easy.
   - Ⓑ People can tape programs to watch at another time.
   - Ⓒ TV programs have become better.
   - Ⓓ People have favorite TV programs.

Name ______________________________ Date ______________

The Dust Bowl

Region tells us the way places in an area are alike. During the 1930s, part of the Great Plains became a region called the Dust Bowl.

When farmers planted wheat, they destroyed the prairie grass that held the soil on the Great Plains. Then came seven years of **drought** in the 1930s. The crops died, and the soil became dry and loose. Wind storms hit the Great Plains and blew dust off the dry fields. Thick dust buried farms, animals, cars, and houses. Dust storms also damaged other areas of the Great Plains.

One effect of the Dust Bowl **disaster** was a renewed effort to **conserve** the soil in the region. To prevent another dust bowl, thousands of trees have been planted to hold down the soil and block the wind on the Great Plains.

Darken the circle by the best answer for each question.

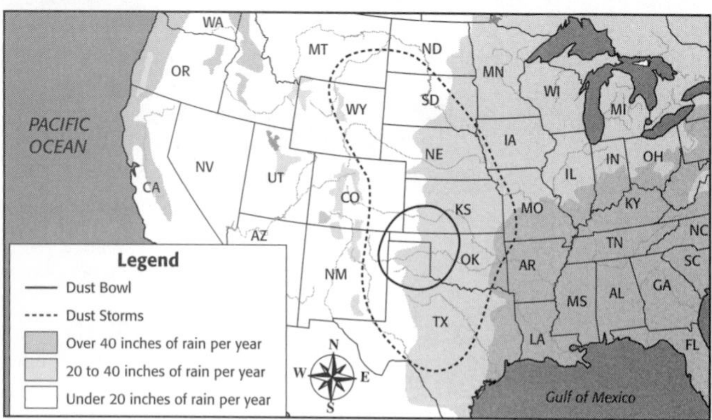

1. Which of these states was not a part of the Dust Bowl?
   Ⓐ Texas
   Ⓑ Oklahoma
   Ⓒ Nebraska
   Ⓓ Kansas

2. After the crops died, _____.
   Ⓐ the farmers planted wheat
   Ⓑ the prairie grass was destroyed
   Ⓒ seven years of drought came
   Ⓓ the soil became dry and loose

3. This article is mainly about _____.
   Ⓐ how to farm in dust
   Ⓑ the causes and effects of the Dust Bowl
   Ⓒ what to do in a dust storm
   Ⓓ how trees hold down the soil

4. From the article, you can tell that a drought is _____.
   Ⓐ a kind of wheat
   Ⓑ a kind of tree
   Ⓒ a long period without rain
   Ⓓ a plow pulled by a mule

Read the paragraphs and study the map of the Dust Bowl. Then write complete sentences to answer the questions.

5. What caused the Dust Bowl? Write a brief summary.

____

____

____

6. What have people in this region done to prevent future dust bowls?

____

____

Name ______________________________ Date ____________

The Declaration of Independence

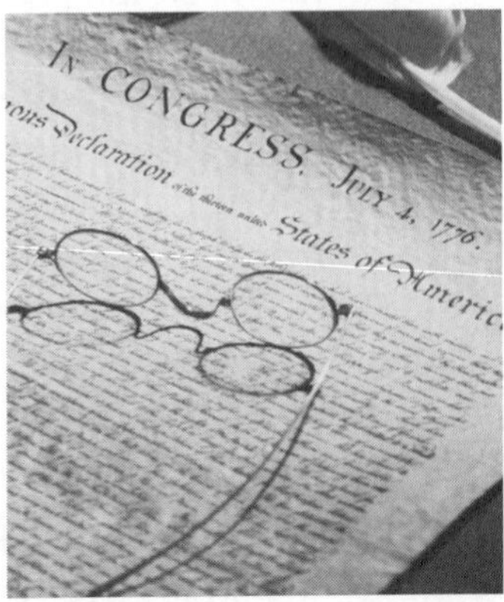

What would cause a group of people to rebel against their homeland and struggle to set up a new nation? By 1776, events in the American colonies had reached a crisis point. A group of men met in Philadelphia that spring and summer, and out of this meeting sprang a new nation. On July 4, 1776, the men officially **adopted** the Declaration of Independence. The document lists several causes for the separation and states that the United States of America is a free and **sovereign** nation. Thomas Jefferson was the primary author of the declaration.

Major parts of the declaration itself can be read in the left column, and a paraphrase is given in the right column.

What the Declaration Says

When in the course of human events, it becomes necessary for one people to dissolve the political bands which have connected them with another, and to assume among the powers of the earth the separate and equal station to which the laws of nature and of nature's God **entitle** them, a decent respect to the opinions of mankind requires that they should declare the causes which **impel** them to the separation.

We hold these truths to be self-evident: that all men are created equal, that they are **endowed** by their Creator with certain **unalienable** rights, that among these are life, liberty, and the pursuit of happiness.

That to secure these rights, governments are instituted among men, **deriving** their just powers from the consent of the governed; that whenever any form of government becomes destructive of these ends, it is the right of the people to alter or to abolish it, and to institute new government, laying its foundation on such principles and organizing its powers in such form as to them shall seem most likely to effect their safety and happiness. **Prudence**, indeed, will dictate that governments long established should not be changed for light and **transient** causes; and accordingly all experience hath shown, that mankind are more disposed to suffer while evils are sufferable, than to right themselves by abolishing the forms to which they are accustomed. But when a long train of abuses and **usurpations**, pursuing invariably the same object, **evinces** a design to reduce them under absolute **despotism**, it is their right, it is their duty, to throw off such government, and to provide new guards for their future security.

What It Means

Sometimes in history, one group of people must become independent from the nation that rules it. The people who are breaking ties must explain their reasons to the world. That is the purpose of this Declaration of Independence.

We believe the following things are always true. All people are equal. God gave all people the natural rights of life, liberty, and working for happiness.

Governments are created by people to protect the people's rights. Governments get their power by the consent of the people they rule. People have the right to change or end a government that takes away their natural rights. The people must then start a new government that will protect natural rights. People should never revolt for a few, unimportant reasons. However, when there is a long history of repeated abuses, then it is the right and the duty of the people to overthrow the ruling government and start a new government that will safeguard the rights of all people.

Name ______________________________ Date ____________

What the Declaration Says	What It Means
Such has been the patient sufferance of these colonies; and such is now the necessity which **constrains** them to alter their former systems of government. The history of the present king of Great Britain is a history of repeated injuries and usurpations, all having in direct object the establishment of an absolute tyranny over these states. To prove this, let facts be submitted to a candid world.	For a long time, the colonies have suffered abuses from the king's government, and so we must change our government. King George, through many unfair actions, has shown that his goals are to take away our rights and to have complete control over the colonies. We want the world to know the following facts about the king's abuses:
He has refused his **assent** to laws, the most wholesome and necessary for the public good. He has forbidden his governors to pass laws of immediate and pressing importance . . . He has refused to pass other laws for the accommodation of large districts of people, unless those people would **relinquish** the right of representation in the legislature, a right **inestimable** to them and **formidable** to tyrants only.	The king has refused to approve laws necessary for the good of the colonies. He has not allowed laws to be passed without his approval. And he has taken a long time to approve those he allows. He has not allowed all people to have equal representation in the legislatures.
He has called together legislative bodies at places unusual, uncomfortable, and distant from the depository of their public records, for the sole purpose of fatiguing them into compliance with his measures. He has dissolved Representative Houses repeatedly, for opposing with manly firmness his invasions on the rights of the people. He has refused for a long time, after such dissolutions, to cause others to be elected; whereby the legislative powers . . . have returned to the people at large for their exercise; . . .	He has forced representatives to meet in strange, uncomfortable, and far-off places in order to make them so tired that they would obey his orders. He has shut down colonial legislatures many times when they criticized the king's abuses of the people. After shutting down legislatures, he has taken a long time before holding new elections. The people are in danger because their colonial governments can not make laws to protect them.
He has endeavored to prevent the population of these states; . . . He has obstructed the administration of justice, by refusing his assent to laws for establishing judiciary powers. He has made judges dependent on his will alone, for the **tenure** of their offices, and the amount and payment of their salaries.	King George has tried to stop the colonial population from growing by making it difficult for Europeans to come to the colonies. He has made it difficult to buy land in America. He stopped us from carrying out justice by refusing to let us set up courts. Judges depend on the king for their salaries and their jobs, so they make unfair decisions to keep their jobs.

Name ______________________________ Date ____________

What the Declaration Says

He has erected a multitude of new offices, and sent hither swarms of officers to harass our people, and eat out their substance.

He has kept among us, in times of peace, standing armies without the consent of our legislatures.

He has affected to **render** the military independent of and superior to the civil power.

What It Means

The king sent large numbers of government people to bother us and use up our resources.

Even in peaceful times, the king has kept his armies in the colonies without the consent of our legislatures.

He has tried to make the military free from, and more powerful than, our government.

What the Declaration Says

He has combined with others to subject us to a jurisdiction . . . unacknowledged by our laws; giving his assent to their acts of pretended legislation:

For quartering large bodies of armed troops among us;

For protecting them, by a mock trial, from punishment for any murders which they should commit on the inhabitants of these states;

For cutting off our trade with all parts of the world;

What It Means

King George has worked with Parliament to give us these unfair laws that we did not help write:

They forced us to allow British soldiers to stay in our homes.

They protected soldiers who murdered our people by giving them fake trials.

They stopped us from trading with other nations.

What the Declaration Says

For imposing taxes on us without our consent;

For depriving us, in many cases, of the benefits of trial by jury;

For transporting us beyond seas to be tried for pretended offenses; . . .

What It Means

They made unfair tax laws for us.

They took away our right to have fair jury trials.

They forced some of our people to go to Great Britain for trials for crimes they never committed.

What the Declaration Says

For taking away our charters, abolishing our most valuable laws, and altering fundamentally the forms of our governments;

For suspending our own legislatures, and declaring themselves **invested** with power to legislate for us in all cases whatsoever;

What It Means

They took away our charters, they changed our most important laws, and they changed the kind of government we have.

They have stopped us from meeting in our legislatures. They say they have the power to make all laws for us.

What the Declaration Says

He has **abdicated** government here, by declaring us out of his protection and waging war against us;

He has plundered our seas, ravaged our coasts, burnt our towns, and destroyed the lives of our people;

He is at this time transporting large armies of foreign **mercenaries** to complete the works of death, desolation, and tyranny, already begun with circumstances of cruelty . . . and totally unworthy of the head of a civilized nation;

What It Means

King George has given up his power to rule us since he says he cannot protect us and is now fighting a war against us.

The king has attacked our ships, destroyed our ports, burned our towns, and destroyed our lives.

He is bringing foreign armies to kill us and destroy the colonies. These soldiers show cruelty that should not be allowed by a modern king.

Name ______________________________ Date____________

What the Declaration Says

He has constrained our fellow citizens taken captive on the high seas to bear arms against their country, to become the executioners of their friends and brethren, or to fall themselves by their hands;

He has excited domestic **insurrections** amongst us, and has endeavored to bring on the inhabitants of our frontiers …

In every stage of these oppressions we have petitioned for **redress** in the most humble terms; our repeated petitions have been answered only by repeated injury. A prince whose character is thus marked by every act which may define a tyrant is unfit to be the ruler of a free people.

Nor have we been wanting in attentions to our British brethren. We have warned them from time to time of attempts by their legislature to extend an **unwarrantable** jurisdiction over us. . . . They too have been deaf to the voice of justice and of **consanguinity**. We must, therefore, **acquiesce** in the necessity which denounces our separation, and hold them, as we hold the rest of mankind, enemies in war, in peace friends.

We, therefore, the representatives of the United States of America, in General Congress assembled, appealing to the Supreme Judge of the world for the **rectitude** of our intentions, do, in the name, and by authority of the good people of these colonies, solemnly publish and declare, that these united colonies are, and of right ought to be, free and independent states; that they are **absolved** from all allegiance to the British crown, and that all political connection between them and the state of Great Britain is, and ought to be, totally dissolved; and that as free and independent states, they have full power to levy war, conclude peace, contract alliances, establish commerce, and to do all other acts and things which independent states may of right do.

And for the support of this declaration, with a firm reliance on the protection of Divine Providence, we mutually pledge to each other our lives, our fortunes and our sacred honor.

What It Means

He has taken Americans off our ships at sea and has forced them to fight against their own people.

He has told our slaves and servants to fight against us, and he has encouraged the Indians to attack us.

We have asked the king to end the unfair treatment of the colonies many times, but each time new abuses were added. A king who acts so unfairly is unfit to rule a free people.

We have hoped the British people would help us end the abuses, so we sent many messages to them. We have told them how Parliament has mistreated us. The British people have not listened to our messages. Therefore, we must declare that we are a separate nation. We will treat Great Britain as we treat all other nations.

As representatives of the people of the United States, we declare that these united colonies are one, independent nation. We have completely cut ties to Great Britain. As an independent nation, we have the right to wage war, make peace treaties, have trade with all nations, and do all the things a nation does.

We now trust that God will protect us. We promise to support this Declaration with our lives, our money, and our honor.

John Hancock (President, Massachusetts)

The declaration was also signed by 56 other men from Georgia, North Carolina, South Carolina, Maryland, Virginia, Pennsylvania, Delaware, New York, New Jersey, Massachusetts, Rhode Island, and Connecticut.

Name ______________________ Date ____________

Comprehension Review

Darken the circle by the best answer.

1. The Declaration of Independence says all people have certain rights, which include life, liberty, and _____.
   Ⓐ a good job
   Ⓑ a nice car
   Ⓒ shelter
   Ⓓ the pursuit of happiness

2. According to the declaration, if a government fails to do what it is set up to do, the people may _____.
   Ⓐ not get to vote
   Ⓑ alter or abolish it
   Ⓒ ask for a refund
   Ⓓ pursue happiness

3. The main idea of the Declaration of Independence is to _____.
   Ⓐ say bad things about King George
   Ⓑ make King George be a better king
   Ⓒ give the reasons the United States should be free from Great Britain
   Ⓓ to tell about some bad laws

4. You can conclude that the men who signed the Declaration of Independence _____.
   Ⓐ were cowards
   Ⓑ really wanted to remain British citizens
   Ⓒ knew many big words
   Ⓓ were willing to die for freedom

Write complete sentences to answer the questions.

5. The Declaration of Independence lists many reasons, or causes, the United States wanted to be independent from Great Britain. Which three of those reasons do you think are the most important? Identify the reasons and explain why they are the most important causes of the Declaration of Independence. Use another piece of paper if necessary.

____

____

____

____

____

____

6. What was the effect of the Declaration of Independence?

____

____

____

Name ______________________________ Date ____________

Vocabulary Review

Darken the circle by the answer that best completes each sentence. Use a dictionary if necessary.

1. King George refused to assent to necessary laws. *To assent* means _____.
   Ⓐ to write
   Ⓑ to approve
   Ⓒ to think about
   Ⓓ to deny

2. King George refused to pass some laws unless the people would relinquish their right of representation. *Relinquish* means _____.
   Ⓐ to link again
   Ⓑ to vote
   Ⓒ to give up
   Ⓓ to enjoy

3. King George sent foreign mercenaries to the colonies. *Mercenaries* are _____.
   Ⓐ tourists
   Ⓑ merchants
   Ⓒ doctors and nurses
   Ⓓ hired soldiers

4. The Declaration of Independence says that people have certain unalienable rights. *Unalienable* means _____.
   Ⓐ not from this world
   Ⓑ can't be taken away
   Ⓒ strange and unusual
   Ⓓ very good

5. The Declaration of Independence says governments should not be changed for transient causes. *Transient* means _____.
   Ⓐ temporary
   Ⓑ homeless
   Ⓒ important
   Ⓓ expensive

6. King George excited insurrections among the colonists. An *insurrection* is _____.
   Ⓐ a kind of musical play
   Ⓑ a law against burying people
   Ⓒ a tax on insurance
   Ⓓ a riot or uprising

7. The Declaration of Independence asks for a blessing of the rectitude of their intentions. *Rectitude* means _____.
   Ⓐ correctness
   Ⓑ wrongness
   Ⓒ a list
   Ⓓ an accident

8. King George abdicated his rule in the colonies. *Abdicated* means _____.
   Ⓐ to make stronger
   Ⓑ to make kinder
   Ⓒ to tax more
   Ⓓ to discard or give up

Choose a vocabulary word from the Declaration of Independence that is not used above. Look up its meaning if you are unsure. Then write a complete sentence using that word.

____

____

____

UNIT 4 Description

Description is concerned with the relationship between the whole and its parts. It can be used to provide physical description, in which details of a person, place, or object are presented to appeal to the reader's senses. It also can be used for division, to identify the component parts that make up the whole of something. In both these forms, the function of description is to demonstrate how the parts work together to produce the whole.

Physical Description (Lesson 11)

Students use physical description on a daily basis to characterize the things around them. They might say, "I ate a juicy orange for lunch" or "The cold ice cream made my tongue tingle" or "We got a new blue car." Each of these descriptions gives physical details about an object. By using these physical details, the writer appeals to the reader's senses. The more of the reader's senses that are brought into play, the more effective is the physical description.

A good physical description will downplay the common features to show the uniqueness of the subject. An assumption is made that all people have two arms or two ears or a nose. Lack of these things would be a kind of uniqueness, or unusual features, such as a long nose, would also be a sign of uniqueness. The details that distinguish one person from another, for example, are the unique features, not the common ones. By showing both common and unique features, description becomes very important in mastering the later skill of classification.

The more thorough the description, the more effectively a sense of the whole is achieved. If a writer says a room has a door and two windows, the reader gets a rough sense of the thing being described. By adding details about the parts, the sense of the whole is more completely realized. As the writer provides more details and a more effective whole, the reader more easily experiences the thing being described.

To get the most information from a physical description:

- First, identify the thing being described (for example, a building).
- Look for details about parts of the thing (for example, doors, windows, walls, roof).
- Look for words that appeal to the senses of sight, smell, taste, touch, and hearing.
- Put all the details together to get the whole picture.
- Try to draw a picture of the thing on paper or in your mind.
- Decide how the thing described is unique or different from other things.
- Try to write a summary description of the thing.

Division–Writing About Parts (Lesson 12)

Like physical description, division is a form of organization that shows how the various parts make up the whole. Division is not the same as classification. Division shows the parts of the whole, whereas classification puts things into different groups. Classification would put the school building into kinds of buildings, but division would discuss the parts of the school building.

Physical description is often a part of division. The parts of the whole are described. However, the main focus of division is to identify the parts that are used to create the whole. You might ask the students, "What are the parts of the classroom?" or "What are the parts of a book?" Using the organizational skill of division, the students can more easily see how the parts work together to create the object.

To get the most information from an article of division:

- First, identify the topic being discussed (for example, the parts of a plant).
- Look for descriptive details about the parts (for example, stem, petals, leaves).
- Pay attention to what each part does in relation to the whole (for example, the stem holds up the plant).
- Put all the parts together to produce the whole thing.
- Try to draw a picture of the thing on paper or in your mind.
- Highlight each part in your picture.
- Try to write a summary that tells how the parts work together to make up the whole thing.

Summary

A summary is a short account of the main idea and key details of an article. A summary should include only the most important points in an article. Key details from the beginning, middle, and end of the article should be included. Readers must sometimes summarize an article when they need to condense the information in an article.

The ability to write a good summary shows the reader's comprehension of the article's main idea and key details.

To summarize an article:

- Read the article carefully, then put it aside.
- Think about the main idea and important details.
- Write the summary without looking at the article.
- Include only the main idea and important details.
- Do include the author's name (if given) and the title of the article.
- Do not use sentences, phrases, or direct quotes from the article.

Physical Description

SELECTION DETAILS

Summary

"Find the Descriptive Details" (page 71): The sample paragraphs give practice in identifying descriptive details in short selections.

"Dolphins and Porpoises" (page 72): This article gives descriptive details about the appearance and behavior of the related dolphins and porpoises.

Selection Type

Science Article

Comprehension Skill

Identify Sensory Words in Descriptive Article

Standards

Reading

- Identify words that appeal to the senses.
- Identify details in a reading selection.

Science

- Based on attributes, place living organisms into groups based on similarities.

VOCABULARY

Introduce the vocabulary words for the article. Write the words on the board. Help students find a definition for each word. Have students use each word in a sentence.

"Dolphins and Porpoises"

streamlined *social*
snouts *pods*

Tap Prior Knowledge

"Dolphins and Porpoises": Ask the students what they know about these popular animals. What is the difference between the two? Have the students draw a picture of each animal.

Skill to Emphasize

Review the section about physical description on page 69. Tell the students that good writers use words that appeal to the reader's senses of sight, smell, taste, touch, and hearing. Sensory words make the writing more interesting and vivid.

Preview Text Features

Point out the title of the article. The titles give the students information about the things that will be described. Have the students look at the illustrations to get a better idea of what is being described. Boldfaced words indicate vocabulary words.

Comprehending the Selection

Model a better understanding of physical description by asking: *What words in the article appeal to your senses of sight, smell, taste, touch, and hearing?*

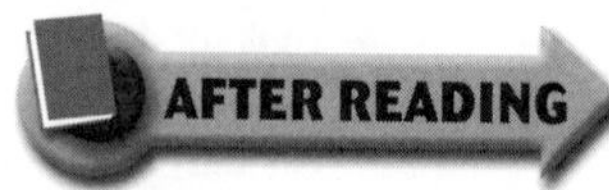

Reinforce the Comprehension Skill

Tell the students that a good description helps them to see an object clearly in their mind. Ask the students to point out words in "Dolphins and Porpoises" that allow them to see pictures clearly in their mind. What are some of the pictures they can see in their mind after reading the article?

Assess

Have the students complete the activities for the selection.

Have the students write a description about a person, place, or thing that they like. Tell them to be sure to use sensory words.

Have the students look for articles in the newspaper or magazines that have detailed descriptions. Have them bring the articles to share with the class.

Name ______________________________ Date____________

Find the Descriptive Details

 **Read each paragraph. Darken the circle by the best answer.**

The red-headed woodpecker lives in areas from Florida to the Canadian border, and ranges as far west as North Dakota. It prefers deciduous woods. Like other woodpeckers, it has a long, sharp bill for digging into trees trunks and a stiff tail. Its boring makes a drumming noise on tree limbs. It has a completely red head and a white patch on its wing that distinguishes it from other woodpeckers. Its call is a raucous *kwrrk*.

1. The red-headed woodpecker has a sharp bill and _____.
   Ⓐ a stiff neck
   Ⓑ a big headache
   Ⓒ no ears
   Ⓓ a stiff tail

2. The red-headed woodpecker has a _____ to distinguish it from other woodpeckers.
   Ⓐ business card
   Ⓑ white patch on its wing
   Ⓒ long, sharp bill
   Ⓓ stiff tail

One of our loveliest trees is the magnolia. It originally comes from Asia. It is named for Pierre Magnol, a French doctor who grew it in his garden. In this country it grows best in the south Atlantic states. It is often seen in the parks and gardens of New York.

The magnolia flower is large and cup-shaped with waxy petals. It is usually purple outside and creamy white inside. Sometimes the blossoms are pure white and very fragrant. These blossoms cannot be shipped by florists because the slightest bruise on the petals makes an ugly, brown mark.

Magnolia leaves are usually dark green, but occasionally a tree is found with glossy purple leaves. These leaves are used by florists for decorations.

3. Magnolia flowers are usually _____.
   Ⓐ brown and ugly
   Ⓑ purple outside
   Ⓒ pure white
   Ⓓ dark green

4. Magnolia leaves are usually _____.
   Ⓐ large and cup-shaped
   Ⓑ pure white and very fragrant
   Ⓒ dark green
   Ⓓ glossy gray

Write complete sentences to answer the question.

5. Why can't magnolia blossoms be shipped by florists? Identify the cause and effect.

____

____

____

____

Name ______________________ Date ____________

Dolphins and Porpoises

Dolphins and porpoises are toothed whales. They have **streamlined** bodies and powerful tails that help them to move easily through the water. Like other whales, dolphins and porpoises have a layer of blubber that keeps them warm.

Dolphins and porpoises are alike in many ways. The main differences in these two mammals is the shape of their snouts and teeth. Dolphins have beaklike snouts and cone-shaped teeth. Porpoises have rounded **snouts** and flat teeth.

Common dolphins grow to be about 7 feet long. They have black backs, gray sides, and white bellies. Common dolphins live in warm waters and often follow ships for miles.

Bottle-nosed dolphins are the most familiar dolphins. They may grow to be 12 feet long. Bottle-nosed dolphins are gray. These dolphins are very **social** and seem to be very friendly toward people.

Killer whales are the largest kind of dolphin. They can grow to be 30 feet long. Killer whales travel in **pods** and are often found in colder northern waters.

Porpoises are smaller than dolphins. The largest porpoises are about 6 feet long. Common porpoises have black backs and white bellies. Unlike dolphins, porpoises avoid people and often travel alone.

Dolphins and porpoises are intelligent animals. They communicate with each other by making chirping sounds. Many dolphins and porpoises live in groups that play and hunt for food together. They help members in the group that are in trouble.

Bottle-Nosed Dolphin

Name ______________________________ Date ______________

Comprehension and Vocabulary Review

Darken the circle by the best answer.

1. Dolphins and porpoises are _____.
   Ⓐ fish
   Ⓑ toothed whales
   Ⓒ not very smart
   Ⓓ red and white

2. Dolphins and porpoises have a layer of _____ that keeps them warm.
   Ⓐ teeth
   Ⓑ wool
   Ⓒ hair
   Ⓓ blubber

3. Dolphins have beaklike _____ and cone-shaped teeth.
   Ⓐ ears
   Ⓑ tails
   Ⓒ snouts
   Ⓓ fins

4. Porpoises have rounded snouts and flat _____.
   Ⓐ feet
   Ⓑ teeth
   Ⓒ babies
   Ⓓ lips

5. _____ are the largest kind of dolphin.
   Ⓐ Killer whales
   Ⓑ Blue whales
   Ⓒ Porpoises
   Ⓓ Tiger sharks

6. Unlike dolphins, porpoises avoid _____ and often travel alone.
   Ⓐ traffic
   Ⓑ eating
   Ⓒ people
   Ⓓ chirping

7. Dolphins and porpoises _____ with each other by making chirping sounds.
   Ⓐ fight
   Ⓑ communicate
   Ⓒ dance
   Ⓓ eat

8. The bottle-nosed dolphin is _____.
   Ⓐ many colors
   Ⓑ black and white
   Ⓒ gray
   Ⓓ unfriendly

Write complete sentences to answer the question.

9. What are two ways that dolphins and porpoises are different in appearance?

____

____

____

____

____

____

Division— Writing About Parts

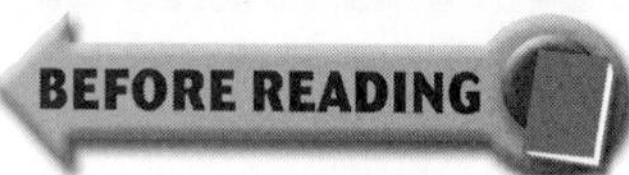

Tap Prior Knowledge

"Atoms": Ask the students if they know what all matter is made of. Do they know what an atom is? Do they know the parts of an atom?

"Parts of the Business Cycle": Ask the students if they have heard people talking about their concerns with the economy. Have they heard the terms *recession* and *depression*? What do these terms mean?

Skill to Emphasize

Review the section about division on page 69. Tell the students that division is a kind of writing that tells about the parts of something. A good division article helps the students to see more easily how the parts work together to make up the object.

Preview Text Features

Point out the title of each article. The titles give the students information about the things that will be divided. Have the students look at the illustrations. The illustrations show the parts that make up the whole. Boldfaced words indicate vocabulary words.

Comprehending the Selection

Model a better understanding of division by asking: *What are the parts that make up the whole?*

Reinforce the Comprehension Skill

Tell the students that a good division article helps them to see how the parts of an object go together to form the whole object. Each part is important and necessary to make the whole.

Assess

Have the students complete the activities for the selection.

Have the students write about something they know that has several parts. Have them identify the whole object, then identify and describe the parts that make up the whole.

Have the students look for instruction manuals that show all the parts of a machine. Have them bring the manuals to school to share with the class.

SELECTION DETAILS

Summary

"Atoms" (page 75): This article discusses the three parts of an atom.

"Parts of the Business Cycle" (page 77): This article identifies the four parts of the business cycle: expansion, peak, recession, and trough.

Selection Type

Science Article
Social Studies Article

Comprehension Skill

Identify Structural Patterns Found in Nonfiction

Standards

Reading

- Identify structural patterns found in nonfiction.
- Identify details in a reading selection.

Science

- Describe elements, compounds, mixtures, atoms and molecules as they relate to matter.

Social Studies

- Describe the factors that cause economic growth in the business cycle.

VOCABULARY

Introduce the vocabulary words for each article. Write the words on the board. Help students find a definition for each word. Have students use each word in a sentence.

"Atoms"

atoms	*electrons*
protons	*nucleus*
neutrons	*electric charges*

"Parts of the Business Cycle"

business cycle	*demand*
expansion	*fiscal policy*
peak	*inflation*
recession	*deflation*
depression	*unemployed*
trough	

Name ________________________________ Date______________

Atoms

Everything is made of **atoms**. Atoms are tiny pieces of matter. They are too small to see even under a microscope. In fact, the smallest piece of matter you can see under a microscope has 10 billion atoms.

Atoms are made of even tinier bits of matter. There are three kinds of particles in atoms. They are **protons**, **neutrons**, and **electrons**. All electrons are exactly the same. All protons are alike, too. So are all neutrons. If all atoms are made of the same kinds of particles, how are atoms different?

Different kinds of atoms are different from each other because they contain a different number of particles. A carbon atom has six protons, six neutrons, and six electrons. Oxygen has eight protons, eight neutrons, and eight electrons. Oxygen is different from carbon because it has more particles. Each kind of atom has a different number of the three particles.

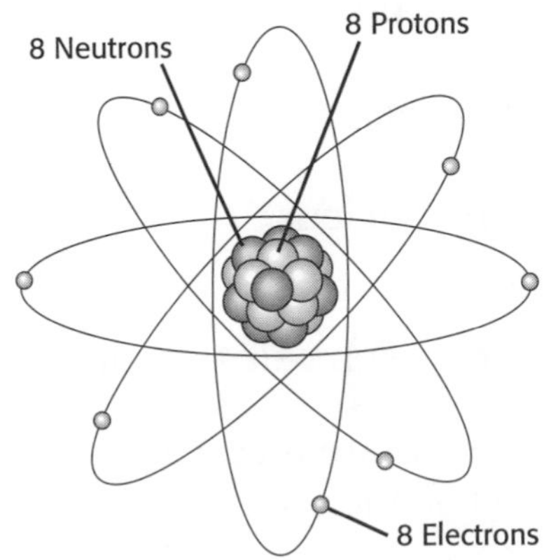

An oxygen atom has 8 positive protons and 8 neutrons in its nucleus, and 8 negative electrons speeding around the nucleus.

Protons and neutrons are in the center, or **nucleus**, of the atom. Electrons are much smaller than protons and neutrons. Electrons move around the nucleus at great speeds. Because electrons move so fast, it is impossible to tell exactly where an electron is at any one time.

The particles that are in atoms have different **electric charges**. Electrons have a negative electric charge. Protons have a positive electric charge. Neutrons have no electric charge. An atom with the same number of electrons and protons also has no electric charge. An atom without an electric charge is called a neutral atom.

Write a complete sentence to answer the question.

What are the three parts of an atom?

____

____

____

____

____

____

____

____

____

Name ______________________ Date __________

Comprehension and Vocabulary Review

Draw lines to complete the sentences.

1. Atoms	have a positive electric charge.
2. Electrons	are made of protons, neutrons, and electrons.
3. Neutrons	have a negative electric charge.
4. Protons	have no electric charge.
5. The nucleus	is made of protons and neutrons.

Darken the circle by the answer that best completes each sentence.

6. Atoms are made of three small _____.
   - Ⓐ elements
   - Ⓑ particles
   - Ⓒ electrons
   - Ⓓ electric charges

7. All electrons are _____.
   - Ⓐ exactly the same
   - Ⓑ positive
   - Ⓒ different
   - Ⓓ slow

8. Different kinds of atoms are different from each other because they contain a different _____ of particles.
   - Ⓐ size
   - Ⓑ number
   - Ⓒ speed
   - Ⓓ charge

9. Protons and neutrons are in the center, or _____, of the atom.
   - Ⓐ nucleus
   - Ⓑ electron
   - Ⓒ charge
   - Ⓓ None of the above

10. Protons have _____.
    - Ⓐ negative charges
    - Ⓑ positive charges
    - Ⓒ changing charges
    - Ⓓ no charge

11. Neutrons have _____.
    - Ⓐ negative charges
    - Ⓑ positive charges
    - Ⓒ changing charges
    - Ⓓ no charge

12. Because electrons _____, it is impossible to tell exactly where an electron is at any one time.
    - Ⓐ move too slowly
    - Ⓑ hop around
    - Ⓒ do not move
    - Ⓓ move so fast

Name ______________________________ Date ______________

Parts of the Business Cycle

The **business cycle** has four parts. Each cycle starts with a time when the economy grows. Businesses sell more and more goods. They may hire new workers. They may build new factories. This part of the business cycle is **expansion**. Expansion is a time of growth in the economy.

After a time of growth, the economy reaches a high point, like the highest place on a roller coaster ride. Unlike a roller coaster, the economy may stay at this high point for months or years. This is a time when almost everyone seems to have money. Jobs are easy to find. Businesses work hard to keep up with demand. Workers may be asked to work longer hours. This part of the business cycle is the **peak**. The peak is the part of the business cycle when business is at its best.

Just as with roller coasters, though, what goes up must come down. After the high point in the business cycle, the economy starts to slide lower. Sales of goods start to fall off. Business slows down. Some workers may lose their jobs. This part of the business cycle is a **recession**. If a recession goes on for a very long time or if it is very bad, it is called a **depression**. During a depression, many businesses may fail. Many people lose their jobs. Most people have little money to spend.

At last the economy reaches its lowest point. This is sometimes called bottoming out. The lowest point in the business cycle is called the **trough**. After each trough comes another expansion. The business cycle then repeats itself.

The Business Cycle

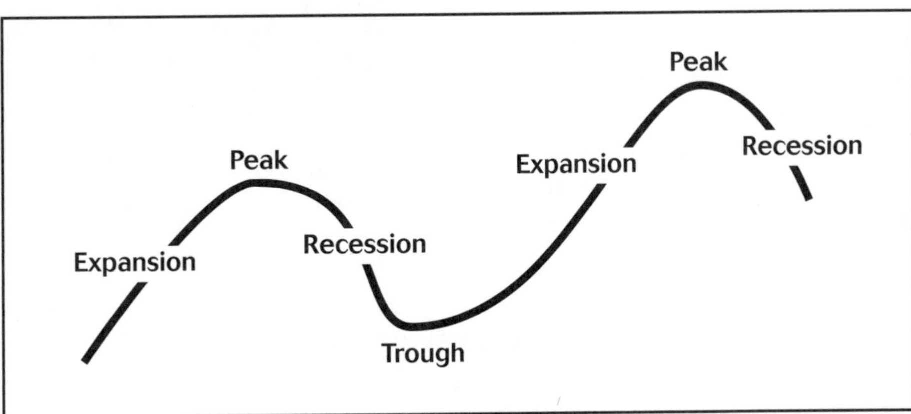

Causes of the Business Cycle

People and how they spend their money are at the heart of the business cycle. The ups and downs of the economy are greatly affected by **demand**. When people buy goods and services, they create demand. High demand causes the expansion of the business cycle. When enough people and businesses spend less, demand falls. Recession results.

Name ______________________________ Date____________

The government's **fiscal policy** can also cause expansion or recession. If the government wants the economy to grow, it can cut taxes, spend more, or both. This policy helps create demand. The government may want the economy to slow down. Raising taxes and cutting spending takes money out of people's pockets. This policy causes demand to fall.

The Business Cycle at Work

We see signs of the business cycle at work in our lives every day. One of the signs we notice first is the price of the things we buy. There are times when the prices of almost all goods and services go up. Such times often happen during the expansion and peak parts of the business cycle. It seems that every time you go to the store, prices are higher. The price of bread, meat, or gasoline may jump every month or every week. When the prices of almost everything are going up, we have **inflation**.

Inflation can be a serious problem. If your pay does not go up as fast as prices of goods and services do, then you will not be able to buy as much. People who get the same amount of money each month are sometimes unable to buy all the things that they need. This often happens to retired people. They get only so much money a month. Inflation also hurts people who have saved money. As prices go up, their money will buy less.

Sometimes prices fall. Such times usually happen during the recession and trough parts of the business cycle. In **deflation**, most things cost less. However, wages may fall, too. Lower prices do not help people, since they have less money to spend. And during a recession, many people may lose their jobs. A person who wants work and cannot find a job is **unemployed**. When many people are out of work, demand for goods and services falls. People have less to spend. Business sales drop. Businesses cut back on production. They may need fewer workers. More people lose their jobs. Sometimes the number of unemployed people becomes very large.

People march to show they want to work.

Write a complete sentence to answer the question.

What are the four parts of the business cycle?

____

____

____

____

____

____

Name ______________________________ Date ______________

Comprehension and Vocabulary Review

Darken the circle by the answer that best completes each sentence.

1. The expansion part of the business cycle is a time of _____.
   Ⓐ slow business
   Ⓑ growth
   Ⓒ recession
   Ⓓ depression

2. When the economy is in recession, it is _____.
   Ⓐ speeding up
   Ⓑ slowing down
   Ⓒ staying the same
   Ⓓ stopping

3. During the peak of the business cycle, workers will have _____ jobs than during a depression.
   Ⓐ more
   Ⓑ fewer
   Ⓒ as many
   Ⓓ worse

4. A very long, bad recession is a _____.
   Ⓐ peak
   Ⓑ trough
   Ⓒ depression
   Ⓓ deflation

5. Inflation is a _____ in the price of almost everything.
   Ⓐ rise
   Ⓑ fall
   Ⓒ stable level
   Ⓓ deflation

6. An unemployed person cannot find _____.
   Ⓐ enough work
   Ⓑ a job
   Ⓒ goods and services
   Ⓓ a depression

Write About It

Use six or more words or phrases in the box to write a summary that tells how the business cycle works. Use another piece of paper if necessary.

demand	**recession**	**spending**	**fiscal policy**
peak	**jobs**	**trough**	**economy**
expansion	**depression**	**growth**	

____

____

____

____

____

UNIT 5 Classification

Classification is concerned with the relationship between a thing and others of its kind. Formal classification is used to classify things, or to place them in groups. This grouping is based on similarities of the things being grouped. Comparison-contrast is used to show the similarities and differences between two things. In both these forms, classification is used to show how one thing is related to other similar things. The details of similarity and contrast are provided by description.

Classification (Lesson 13)

Students are involved with classification on a daily basis. They are grouped according to their gender, their school grade, and their family associations. They watch TV shows grouped by kind, study groups of subjects in school, and play different kinds of sports. Classification is a skill that students learn early in their school life. They may be asked to group shapes according to color or size, for example. They may be asked to identify their favorite food or color.

The process of classification moves from general to specific. A tree diagram is helpful for illustrating this concept; one is provided on page 122. The first level of classification is a very general group, such as Fruits. The next level of classification is more specific. The names of specific fruits are added to the diagram, such as apples, oranges, bananas, and grapes. Then, very specific descriptive details about each fruit are added to the diagram. These details can be used later for comparison-contrast of two fruits.

A tree diagram can have many levels, depending on the needs of the classification. For example, the classification of Fruits could add extra levels. Instead on naming only fruits under the general heading, one could add extra subheadings of kinds of fruits, such as Citrus Fruits and Tropical Fruits. Then, specific fruits could be added to these subheadings, and specific details could be provided for each fruit.

To identify the groups in a classification:

- Use the Classification Tree Diagram on page 122.
- First identify the general group (for example, kinds of pets).
- Then identify any subgroups under the general group (for example, kinds of dogs).
- Then identify the specific members of the general group or subgroup.
- Identify the specific details about each member.
- Think about why the specific members belong in the general group.
- You might want to distribute a tree diagram and allow the students to perform a classification before reading the selections. A common topic such as Snacks or Sports would be a good place to start.

Comparison-Contrast (Lesson 14)

Students can easily relate to the concept of comparison-contrast by introducing it using the terms *alike* and *different*. How are two games alike? How are they different? However, comparison-contrast works well only if the two items are from a common category. For example, comparing and contrasting two kinds of food is logical. Comparing and contrasting a banana and a brick is not really logical.

Comparison-contrast is used to show the similarities and differences between things. *Compare* means to show how things are alike. *Contrast* means to show how things are different. If possible, a comparison-contrast should be limited to two items. Three points of comparison-contrast should be used. For example, two people could be compared and contrasted based on their height, weight, and shoe size. The details about group members in a Tree Diagram are useful in comparing and contrasting.

A Venn Diagram is a useful tool for comparing and contrasting. A Venn Diagram is provided on page 123. The Venn Diagram graphically represents the similarities and differences. The differences are placed in the outer parts of the ovals. The similarities are placed where the two ovals intersect. You might want to distribute a Venn Diagram and allow the students to perform a comparison-contrast before reading the selections. A simple comparison-contrast of apples and oranges would be a good starting point.

To get the most information from a comparison-contrast:

- Use the Venn Diagram on page 123.
- First identify the two things being compared and contrasted.
- Then identify the points used to compare and contrast the two things.
- Think about the ways the things are alike and different.
- Often, the writer is trying to show that one thing is better than another. So be aware of any attempt to persuade the reader.

Graphic Organizers

LESSON 13

Classification

SELECTION DETAILS

Summary

"Kinds of Rocks" (page 82): Classifies the three general kinds of rocks.

"Poisonous Plants" (page 83): Classifies the two kinds of poisonous plants.

"Kinds of Economic Systems" (page 85): Classifies the four kinds of economic systems.

Selection Type

Science Articles
Social Studies Article

Comprehension Skill

Identify Classification in a Nonfiction Article

Standards

Reading

- Use reading strategies (classification) to comprehend text.
- Identify structural patterns found in nonfiction.
- Identify details in a reading selection.

Science

- Explain the processes involved in the formation of the Earth's structure.
- Arrange several organisms into a classification system.

Economics

- Describe the characteristics of production and exchange in an economic cycle.

VOCABULARY

"Kinds of Rocks"
igneous, metamorphic, sedimentary, sediments

"Poisonous Plants"
poisonous, adaptation

"Kinds of Economic Systems"
economic system, traditional economy, command economy, factors of production, market economy, market, mixed economy

Tap Prior Knowledge

"Kinds of Rocks": Ask the students if they know the three kinds of rocks. What are examples of each kind?

"Poisonous Plants": Ask the students if they have ever gotten into poison ivy or some other plant. What happened?

"Kinds of Economic Systems": Ask the students to name the kind of economic system in the United States. What kind of economic system might be found in a communist country?

Skill to Emphasize

Review the section about classification on page 80. Tell the students that writers often put things in groups to help the reader to identify them more easily.

Preview Text Features

Have the students look at the illustrations in the "Kinds of Rocks" and "Poisonous Plants" articles. They help the students to envision the kinds of rocks and poisonous plants. Boldfaced words indicate vocabulary words.

Comprehending the Selection

Model a better understanding of classification by asking: *What general group of things is being discussed? What are the individual members of that group?*

Reinforce the Comprehension Skill

Tell the students that a good classification helps them to understand the common features between groups of things. Ask the students to point out the members of each group named in the title of the article. Distribute copies of the Classification Tree Diagram on page 122 to help the students organize the information.

Assess

Have the students complete the activities for the selection.

Distribute copies of the Classification Tree Diagram on page 122. Have the students choose a general group to classify. Have them include at least three individual members of that group. They should also include details about each individual member. Then, have them write a short classification essay using the information they have compiled in their tree diagram.

Name ______________________________ Date ______________

Kinds of Rocks

Rocks are all around you. They form the crust of the Earth itself. People use rocks for many things. They climb them, they collect them, they build things with them, and they even wear them. Rocks change. They break down, melt, change shape, harden, and soften. Rocks are found in three forms: **igneous**, **metamorphic**, and **sedimentary**.

Igneous rocks are formed when red-hot melted rock cools down. Where would you find red-hot melted rock? It is deep inside the Earth. Sometimes this melted rock comes to the surface as the lava that flows from volcanoes. Granite is a kind of igneous rock.

Sedimentary rocks are formed when tiny bits of rocks are worn away. The bits, called **sediments**, are washed away by rain and snow. The sediments settle in streams and river beds, as well as on the ocean floor. Over a long time, the sediments harden to form rock. An example of a sedimentary rock is sandstone.

Sometimes rocks get buried deep inside the Earth. These buried rocks could be of any type: igneous, metamorphic, or sedimentary. The heat and pressure deep within the Earth change the rocks that are buried there. Rocks that have been changed from one form to another are called metamorphic rocks. Slate is a metamorphic rock.

Darken the circle by the best answer.

1. Rocks are found in three forms: igneous, metamorphic, and _____.
   Ⓐ slate
   Ⓑ sedimentary
   Ⓒ granite
   Ⓓ polished

2. When melted rock cools, it is called _____.
   Ⓐ igneous rock
   Ⓑ sedimentary rock
   Ⓒ metamorphic rock
   Ⓓ soft rock

3. Igneous rock is changed to sedimentary rock after it has been _____.
   Ⓐ melted
   Ⓑ exposed to high heat and pressure
   Ⓒ worn away by water and wind
   Ⓓ put in a blender

4. Sandstone is an example of _____ rock.
   Ⓐ sedimentary
   Ⓑ igneous
   Ⓒ metamorphic
   Ⓓ slate

Write a complete sentence to answer the question.

5. What are the three forms, or kinds, of rock?

____

____

Name ______________________________ Date ____________

Poisonous Plants

For some plants, being **poisonous** is a special **adaptation**. Because of this poison, people and animals learn to stay away from these plants. There are two kinds of poisonous plants. One kind has an effect on the skin of people who touch the plant. The other kind is harmful to people or animals if they eat the plant.

Poison Ivy

If you touch poison ivy, an oil from the plant can give you an itchy rash. Poison ivy grows in woods and fields. It can form a vine that wraps around trees or other plants. Poison ivy has shiny green leaves in groups of three. The plant also has small green flowers and berries. Poison oak and poison sumac are other plants that give people itchy rashes. It is important to learn what these plants look like so you can avoid them. If you do touch them, wash your skin with soap and water right away.

Mushrooms

Other plants are harmful if they are eaten. Some mushrooms that grow wild are poisonous. Never eat a mushroom that you find growing. Even tasting a small piece of a poisonous mushroom can be dangerous. Many garden plants are poisonous if eaten. The flowers of the lily-of-the-valley plant are poisonous. So are daffodils. All parts of azalea plants are poisonous.

Even some parts of food plants are poisonous. You can eat the stems of the rhubarb plant. But there is poison in the leaves. Eating rhubarb leaves can make you sick.

Daffodils

Name ______________________________ Date ____________

Comprehension and Vocabulary Review

Darken the circle by the answer that best completes each sentence.

1. People and animals learn to stay away from _____ plants.
   Ⓐ broccoli
   Ⓑ poisonous
   Ⓒ red
   Ⓓ garden

2. Some plants can give you an itchy rash when you _____ them.
   Ⓐ look at
   Ⓑ smell
   Ⓒ touch
   Ⓓ eat

3. Some mushrooms that grow wild are poisonous to _____.
   Ⓐ cook
   Ⓑ harvest
   Ⓒ touch
   Ⓓ eat

4. For some plants, being poisonous is _____.
   Ⓐ an adaptation
   Ⓑ an effect
   Ⓒ a way to get even
   Ⓓ fun

Write complete sentences to answer the questions.

5. Poisonous plants are classified according to the effect they cause. What are the two effects used to classify poisonous plants?

____

____

____

6. How do you think being poisonous helps a plant?

____

____

7. What are two poisonous plants that produce a rash on the skin?

____

____

8. What is a poisonous plant that is dangerous to eat?

____

____

Name ______________________________ Date ______________

Kinds of Economic Systems

Every nation must answer three questions about goods and services. These questions are called the three basic questions of economics:

1. What goods and services should be produced?
2. How should these goods and services be produced?
3. Who will get the goods and services?

How a country answers the three basic economic questions tells a great deal about that country. Each country has an **economic system**. An economic system is the rules a country follows in answering the three basic questions. There are four kinds of economic systems.

A **traditional economy** makes decisions based on what has been done in the past. People produce the goods and services they have always produced. People may herd cattle because their family has always herded cattle. One village may produce clay pots because people who live there have always made them. The question "How should goods and services be produced?" is answered in the same way. If a girl's mother made rugs with a particular pattern, the girl will make the same kind of rugs using the same methods. People in this kind of economy usually share equally in the goods and services provided. Thus, the answer to the third question is "Everyone gets the same amount."

In a **command economy**, government leaders decide the answers to the basic economic questions. The government controls the land, labor, and capital, the three **factors of production**. The government decides what and how much of each item will be made. It decides where people will work, whether they will use machines or do work by hand, and how much they will be paid. Finally, the government decides who will be able to buy the goods and services that are produced.

Name ____________________ Date __________

A **market economy** is the opposite of a command economy. In a market economy, each person answers the three basic questions. People may buy and sell whatever they like. People decide for themselves whether they will make things by hand or by machine.

The most important part of a market economy is the **market**. A market is the means by which goods and services are bought and sold freely. For example, a person who has an item for sale is free to sell it to anyone who will buy it. In a market system, therefore, people usually produce goods that other people will want to buy. This answers the question of what to produce. How goods will be produced is up to the person making them. One person may make tables by hand while another may make them using machines. Who gets the goods depends on who is willing and able to buy them. The person who wants a cheap table may buy one made by machine. The person who wants a table that is not like any other may buy one made by hand.

Most nations in the world today have a **mixed economy**. A mixed economy is one which is part command and part market economy. Most governments have some say over how the three basic economic questions are answered. However, many decisions are left up to the people. The United States has a mixed economy.

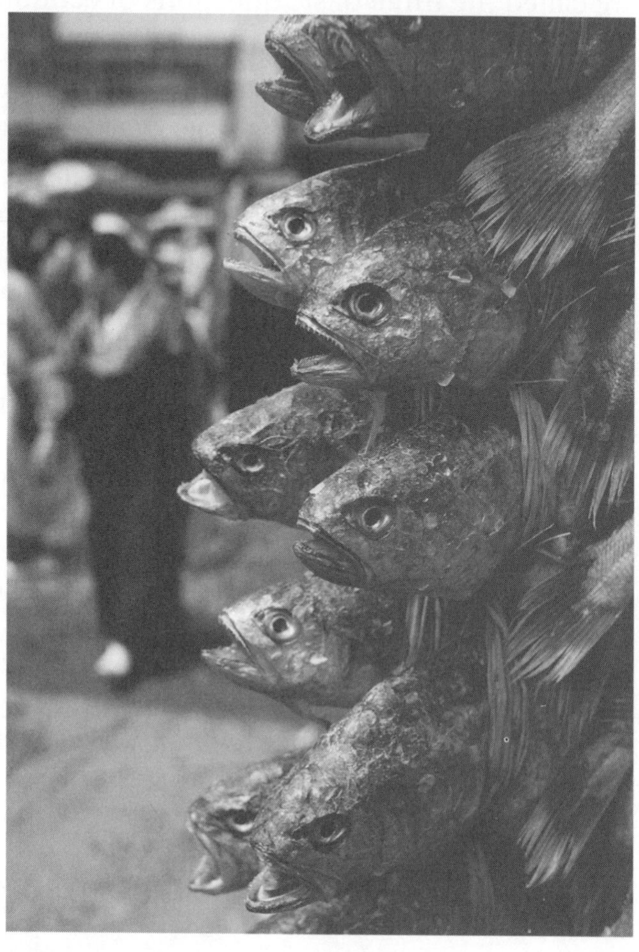

Dried fish in Asian market

 **Write complete sentences to answer the question.**

What are the four economic systems discussed in the article?

____

____

____

____

____

____

____

____

Name ______________________________ Date ______________

Comprehension and Vocabulary Review

Darken the circle by the best answer.

1. The rules a country follows in answering questions about what to produce, how to produce it, and who gets it make up that country's _____.
   Ⓐ three basic questions
   Ⓑ economic system
   Ⓒ market
   Ⓓ factors of production

2. Decisions in a _____ are based on what has been done in the past.
   Ⓐ traditional economy
   Ⓑ command economy
   Ⓒ market economy
   Ⓓ mixed economy

3. People may make, buy, and sell whatever they like in a _____.
   Ⓐ traditional economy
   Ⓑ command economy
   Ⓒ market economy
   Ⓓ mixed economy

4. Government leaders decide the answers to the three basic questions in a _____.
   Ⓐ traditional economy
   Ⓑ command economy
   Ⓒ market economy
   Ⓓ mixed economy

5. Most nations today have a _____.
   Ⓐ traditional economy
   Ⓑ command economy
   Ⓒ market economy
   Ⓓ mixed economy

6. _____ is the means by which goods and services are bought and sold freely.
   Ⓐ An economy
   Ⓑ A command economy
   Ⓒ A factor of production
   Ⓓ A market

Write About It

Use four or more words or phrases in the box to write a paragraph that explains how a command economy and a market economy are different. Use another piece of paper if necessary.

government	**factors of production**	**goods**
market	**command**	**services**
control	**economy**	**three basic questions**

____

____

____

____

____

LESSON 14

Comparison-Contrast

SELECTION DETAILS

Summary

"Hibernation" (page 89): This article uses a chart to compare and contrast the body changes in several animals during hibernation.

"Air Masses" (page 90): This article compares and contrasts the actions and effects of cold and warm air masses.

"Kachinas" (page 91): This article compares and contrasts three kachinas involved in American Indian ceremonies.

"Comparing Climate and Population Maps" (page 92): This article allows students to compare and contrast population in relation to climate in an area.

Selection Type

Science Articles
Social Studies Articles

Comprehension Skill

Identify Comparison-Contrast in a Nonfiction Article

Standards

Reading

- Understand the use of comparison and contrast in a nonfiction selection.
- Demonstrate a basic understanding of culturally diverse written texts.

Science

- Know adaptations that allow animals to survive

Social Studies

- Determine how ancient cultures and religions affect present-day people.

VOCABULARY

"Hibernation"
hibernate

"Air Masses"
air mass
front
cold front
warm front
stationary front

"Kachinas"
pueblos
kachinas
ceremonial

Tap Prior Knowledge

"Hibernation": Ask the students if they know of any animals that hibernate. Why do these animals hibernate?

"Air Masses": Ask the students if they know what causes wind or storms. Do they know what a cold front is?

"Kachinas": Ask the students what they know about Southwestern American Indian culture. Kachinas are religious symbols. Can they think of any other symbols used in religion?

"Comparing Climate and Population Maps": Ask the students why they think people live where they do. Do they think weather can be one cause?

Skill to Emphasize

Review the section about comparison-contrast on page 80. Tell the students that *compare* means to show how things are alike and *contrast* means to show how things are different.

Preview Text Features

Point out the chart in ""Hibernation." It gives information about four animals' body rates during hibernation. The diagrams in "Air Masses" show the movement of air in each kind of air mass. The illustrations in "Kachinas" help the students to envision the symbolic characters. The two maps in "Comparing Climate and Population Maps" show the relationship between climate and population in Australia. Boldfaced words indicate vocabulary words.

Comprehending the Selection

Model a better understanding of comparison-contrast by asking: *In what ways are the two things alike and different?*

Reinforce the Comprehension Skill

Tell the students that comparison-contrast helps them to understand how two things are alike and different. The two things are of the same general group, so they have basic common features. The differences are what allow the students to tell one thing from the other. Distribute copies of the Venn diagram on page 123 to help the students organize the information.

Assess

Have the students complete the activities for the selection.

Name ______________________ Date ____________

Hibernation

In winter, food is hard to find in cold places. To avoid starving to death, some animals migrate. Others stay in the area. These animals first store up food in the form of body fat. Next, they find a safe place to spend the winter. Finally, they fall into a long, deep sleep. They sleep, or **hibernate**, through the cold winter and awake when the weather turns warmer.

When an animal hibernates, its body temperature drops and its heartbeat slows. The chart below shows body changes for four animals during hibernation.

BODY CHANGES DURING HIBERNATION

ANIMAL	AWAKE		IN HIBERNATION	
	Body Temperature	Heartbeats per Minute	Body Temperature	Heartbeats per Minute
Woodchuck	39° C	80–120	16° C	3–10
Ground squirrel	39° C	200–400	4° C	2–10
Brown bat	40° C	400–700	2° C	7–10
Hamster	35° C	200–400	6 ° C	4–12

 **Write a complete sentence to answer each question.**

1. How fast does a ground squirrel's heart beat during hibernation?

____

____

2. How fast does a brown bat's heart beat when it is awake?

____

____

3. Which two animals have the same heartbeat rate when they are not hibernating?

____

____

4. Which animal's body temperature remains the highest during hibernation?

____

____

Name ______________________ Date ____________

Air Masses

A large body of air with the same temperature, pressure, and humidity is called an **air mass**. Air masses are produced when air remains over one part of the Earth's surface for a long time. These great air masses move slowly across the Earth's surface. These moving air masses take on the characteristics of the surface beneath them. Air moving over a warm surface is warmed, and air moving over a cold surface is cooled. Air moving over water becomes moist, and air moving over land becomes drier. As it moves, the air mass causes changes in the weather of an area.

A **front** is a line or boundary between air masses. The passage of a front usually produces changes in temperature, pressure, wind speed and direction, and humidity. The air masses clash along the front, so weather along a front is often stormy. A **cold front** occurs when a cold air mass replaces a warm air mass. Weather along a cold front often includes thunderstorms with much precipitation.

A **warm front** occurs when a warm air mass replaces a cold air mass. Precipitation may also occur along a warm front, but the precipitation is usually not as heavy as along a cold front. A **stationary front** occurs when air masses meet without moving. A stationary front may produce an extended period of precipitation.

Cold Front　　Warm Front

Write complete sentences to answer the questions.

1. What characteristics do all air masses have in common?

____

____

2. What is a characteristic of an air mass over land?

____

____

3. What three kinds of fronts can form between air masses?

____

____

4. How is a cold front different from a warm front?

____

____

Name ______________________ Date ____________

Kachinas

The American Indians of the Southwest were farmers. Many of these tribes lived in large communities called **pueblos**. Their religious celebrations centered on the growing of crops. **Kachinas**, the messengers of the Pueblo Indians' gods, were an important part of the celebrations. Some tribe members took on the personality of different kachinas. They wore **ceremonial** masks and colorful costumes. These traditions still exist today.

Sun Kachina
Visits Hopi villages during the bean-planting ceremony. Appeals to the Sun for health, happiness, long life, and good crops.

Clown Kachina
Appears during most ceremonies to entertain the crowd. Performs acrobatics, tells jokes, and leads games. Is noisy and silly.

Kachina Mother
Leads the bean-planting ceremony. Is actually a male performer.

Study the paragraph and the drawings. Write complete sentences to answer the questions.

1. Which kachina is a spirit of nature? ______________________

2. How can you tell one kind of kachina from another? ______________________

____

3. Which part of the Sun Kachina's costume represents the Sun? Explain.

____

____

4. Which kachina do you think would play the most important role at the bean-planting ceremony? Explain. ______________________

____

____

____

____

Name ______________________ Date __________

Comparing Climate and Population Maps

A climate map tells about the average weather in an area over a period of time. A population map shows how many people live in an area. You can learn basic information about Australia by comparing the population and climate maps on this page. The climate map shows a temperate, or mild, climate in the southeast. By comparing the two maps, you can see that more people live in the southeast where there is a temperate climate.

Study the two maps. Finish each sentence in Group A with an answer from Group B. Write the letter for the correct answer on the line.

Group A	**Group B**
1. Most of Australia has a ____ climate.	A. Darwin
2. Perth and Adelaide have a ____ climate.	B. 0–2
3. Australia has ____ cities with a temperate climate.	C. temperate
4. Alice Springs has ____ people per square mile.	D. desert
5. Some interior desert areas have ____.	E. no people
6. ____ has a tropical climate.	F. tropical
7. The highest population density is in the temperate and ____ climates.	G. four

Population Map of Australia

INDONESIA
Darwin
Coral Sea
Alice Springs
AUSTRALIA
Brisbane
Perth
Adelaide
Sydney
Canberra
INDIAN OCEAN
Melbourne
Tasman Sea
Hobart

MAP KEY
Persons per square mile
0–2
2–10
More than 10

Climate Map of Australia

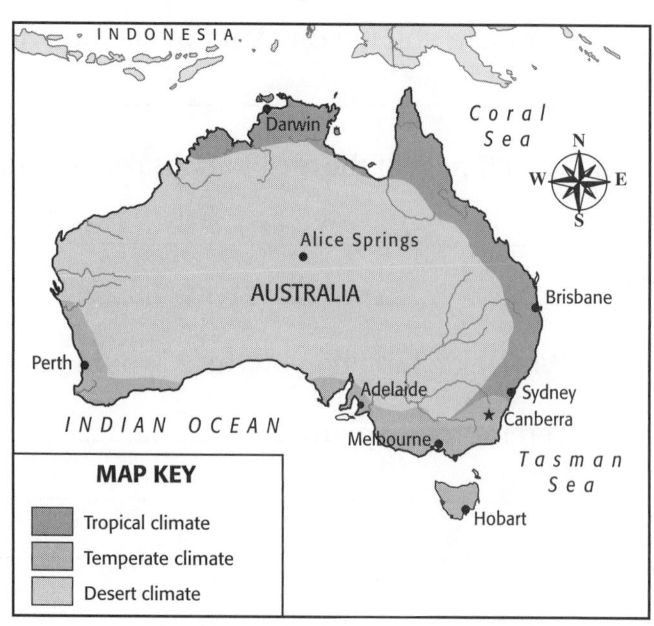

UNIT 6 Conclusion

Sometimes an author may not tell the reader directly what is happening in an article. Sometimes the reader must make a conclusion based on the facts of the article or the reader's own experiences or observations. After making a conclusion, the reader may need to change it if additional facts and details are gathered. Sometimes the reader must also determine the writer's purpose or conclude if a writer's statement is a fact or an opinion.

Drawing Conclusions (Lesson 15)

A conclusion is a logical judgment based on a set of facts. If there are mud tracks on the carpet, one can logically conclude that the person with mud on his or her shoes made those tracks. New facts may cause the conclusion to be incorrect, but the conclusion is reasonable based on the facts that are available. In drawing conclusions, the reader must pay attention to all the facts. A conclusion is not logical or valid if it is based on only some of the facts; a good conclusion is based on all of the facts.

However, one cannot say that there is only one conclusion for a set of facts. Many conclusions can be drawn from a set of facts, and they can all be reasonable and valid. Only as new facts are gathered do some of the conclusions become invalid.

To draw logical conclusions:

- Read the information carefully.
- Think about the facts and your own experiences and observations.
- Decide what all the facts tell you.
- Write a conclusion based on the facts you have available.
- Be sure your conclusion uses all the facts, not just some.
- Change your conclusion if new facts show something different.

Fact or Opinion? (Lesson 16)

Nonfiction articles contain facts. Nonfiction articles sometimes also give opinions, or a person's beliefs. Facts are used to inform, and opinions are used to persuade. Sometimes a reader must decide, or conclude, if a statement is a fact or an opinion. Writers often use facts to support their opinions. They want to convince the reader that what they are claiming is true. If an article contains opinions, the writer is probably trying to persuade the reader.

Facts can be used to prove an issue. Opinions cannot prove anything. An opinion is simply a person's belief, often not supported by facts of any kind. The opinion is just what that person thinks, right or wrong. Facts are considered always to be right.

How to distinguish facts from opinions:

- Use the Fact-Opinion Chart on page 124.
- Facts can be proven, but opinions cannot be proven.
- When you read a statement, ask yourself, "Can this statement be proven?" If the answer is yes, it is a fact. If the answer is no, it is an opinion.
- The words *should, must, think,* and *believe* are often clues that a sentence is an opinion.
- Make a mental note that a statement is a fact or an opinion.
- If you must make a logical conclusion, use only facts, not opinions.

Purpose and Structure (Lesson 17)

Students must sometimes also determine a writer's purpose for writing. Personal writing tells something about the writer or how the writer feels about something. Literary writing tells a story or a poem and is usually fictional. Persuasive writing tries to make the readers change their minds about some issue, often by using facts. Referential writing simply tells facts about a topic without trying to convince the reader. Sometimes a referential writer will interpret the facts and draw logical conclusions. The reader must decide which of these purposes the writer has used.

A writer accomplishes purpose through structure. The writer chooses certain organizational structures to communicate the information in the best possible way. Students have studied many of these organizational structures in this book: narration, cause-effect, description, division, classification, and comparison-contrast. A student is best able to analyze a writing through the writer's purpose and structure.

How to determine purpose and structure:

- Find the main idea and key details.
- Why did the writer want to accomplish that main idea? (purpose)
- How did the writer accomplish the main idea? (structure)

Graphic Organizer

Fact-Opinion Chart page 124

LESSON 15

Conclusion

Tap Prior Knowledge

"Steven Spielberg": Ask the students if they have ever seen *Jaws*, *E.T.*, or *Jurassic Park*. Those movies were directed by Steven Spielberg. What do they think this man might be like?

"Japan: Industrial Leader of Asia": Ask the students if they own anything made in Japan. The possibility is great. Ask the students what else they know about Japan, including historical relations with the United States.

Skill to Emphasize

Review the section about drawing conclusions on page 93. Tell the students that writers sometimes do not tell the reader everything that is happening in an article. The reader sometimes must draw conclusions, or make judgments, about the facts given.

Preview Text Features

Have the students look at the illustrations and map in "Japan: Industrial Leader of Asia." The illustrations show common images of Japan. The map shows the geographical location of Japan in the Pacific Ocean. Boldfaced words indicate vocabulary words.

Comprehending the Selection

Model a better understanding of conclusion by asking: *Using the facts given, what conclusions can you make about the topic?*

Reinforce the Comprehension Skill

Tell the students that a good conclusion is based on all the facts of the article. They should be sure their conclusions make sense and include all the facts.

Assess

Have the students complete the activities for the selection.

Have the students write a paragraph telling why they think history is or is not an important thing to know about.

SELECTION DETAILS

Summary

"Draw a Conclusion" (page 95): The sample paragraphs give practice in drawing conclusions in short selections.
"Steven Spielberg" (page 97): This article briefly narrates the childhood and career success of this noted film director.
"Japan: Industrial Leader of Asia" (page 99): This article discusses geography, history, culture, and economics of Japan.

Selection Type

Social Studies Articles

Comprehension Skill

Draw Conclusions from Facts in a Nonfiction Article

Standards

Reading

- Make and explain inferences from texts such as drawing conclusions.
- Demonstrate a basic understanding of culturally diverse written texts.

Social Studies

- Put in chronological order important people and events.
- Identify common characteristics of regions at local, national, and international scales on the basis of climate, landforms, ecosystems, and culture.

VOCABULARY

Introduce the vocabulary words and write them on the board. Help students find a definition for each word. Have students use each word in a sentence.

"Steven Spielberg"

techniques *enchanted*
motto

"Japan: Industrial Leader of Asia"

archipelago *balance of trade*
kimonos *terraces*
bonsai *constitutional monarchy*

Name ______________________ Date __________

Draw a Conclusion

To draw a conclusion, you need to see how information fits together and gives an article meaning. To draw a correct conclusion, you must be sure it is supported by the article.

Read each article and draw a conclusion based on the facts. Darken the circle by the best answer.

At one time, people in the United States got most of the things they needed from within the country. Oranges came from Florida, Texas, or California. Lumber came from Oregon. Most clocks, watches, and shoes came from the New England states. Automobiles came from Detroit, Michigan.

Today we get food and supplies from all over the world. Cars can come from Japan. We import shoes from Brazil, Korea, and China. Many of the clothes we wear are made in the Far East or Balkan countries.

1. What conclusion can you draw from this selection?
   Ⓐ Shoes are manufactured in New England.
   Ⓑ Japanese cars are very good.
   Ⓒ We get things we need from all over the world.
   Ⓓ We need oranges.

After World War I, new immigration laws were passed. In 1917, a law was passed specifying 33 classes of foreigners who could not be admitted to the United States. Immigrants who were admitted had to pass a literacy test. This new law greatly reduced the number of immigrants for a while, but by 1921 the number of arrivals again climbed to 500,000. New, stricter laws were enacted in 1921 and again in 1924. Organizations like the Immigration Restriction League and labor groups supported these laws.

2. What conclusion can you draw from this selection?
   Ⓐ Literacy tests are important.
   Ⓑ There are many classes of foreigners.
   Ⓒ We need new, stricter immigration laws.
   Ⓓ Some organizations wanted to reduce the number of immigrants.

Before railroads or automobiles, carriages were used to transport people. They were similar to cars, but they didn't have motors. Carriages were pulled by horses, donkeys, or mules. During the Middle Ages in Europe, carriages were not used very often. The roads were unpaved and usually in very poor condition. Carriages gained popularity once new roads were built. During their time, carriages provided useful and convenient transportation.

3. What conclusion can you draw from this selection?
   Ⓐ Carriages didn't have motors.
   Ⓑ Good roads were important for carriage travel.
   Ⓒ Carriage transportation was popular.
   Ⓓ There were many unpaved roads.

Name ________________________________ Date______________

Read each article and draw a conclusion based on the facts. Darken the circle by the best answer.

Thousands of years ago, the native people of India far outnumbered their conquerors. In order to keep control over the native people, the conquerors invented a plan called the caste system. The conquerors belonged to the highest class. The natives belonged to the lower classes. There were special rules which had to be followed. No person of one caste could eat with a member of another caste. No one could marry into another caste. Anyone who broke the rules was severely punished. The caste system in India was practiced by Hindus. Most high-caste Hindus thought that they couldn't come near the lowest caste, who were known as untouchables. They thought it would make them impure.

4. What conclusion can you draw from this selection?
Ⓐ Native Indians like the caste system.
Ⓑ The caste system kept people down.
Ⓒ Caste system rules are fair.
Ⓓ It is easy to conquer other people.

Whales are found in all the oceans of the world. Some whales live in very deep water, so they are rarely seen. Other whales live near the shore where they can be seen often. Whales travel from place to place during different times of the year. Part of the year they feed in the cold waters near the North and South Poles. Whales travel to warmer waters to have their babies.

5. What conclusion can you draw from this selection?
Ⓐ Whales are hard to find.
Ⓑ Some whales are shy.
Ⓒ All whales prefer deep water.
Ⓓ None of the above

Read the paragraph below and the sentences that follow it. Put a check before the conclusions that can be drawn from the paragraph.

In a command economy, the government owns the land and the factories. It tells the workers where they must work. It tells people how much of each item to make. Government decides how much people will be paid. It even controls who can buy goods and services.

_____ **a.** People do not have much economic freedom in a command economy.

_____ **b.** A person cannot change jobs unless the government says so.

_____ **c.** People do not like to live in a command economy.

_____ **d.** Government controls mean that everyone may have an equal chance to buy goods and services.

Name ______________________________ Date ______________

Steven Spielberg

Do you want to be a successful movie director like Steven Spielberg? You'd better get started—now! The Oscar-winning creator of such fantastic movies as *Jaws*, *E.T*, *Saving Private Ryan*, and *Jurassic Park* was charging admission to his homemade movies when he was just twelve. According to one viewer, the young Spielberg's movies were full of clever **techniques**.

Childhood memories echo throughout Spielberg's thoughts and his movies. He remembers seeing a movie about Davy Crockett when he was eight. Davy said, "Be sure you're right, and then go ahead." This became Spielberg's **motto**. He's never stopped working to turn his dreams into successful realities.

Spielberg also remembers when his father took him to see a meteor shower. At first, young Steven was scared to be wakened in the middle of the night. Then the beautiful lights **enchanted** him. The mystery of outer space became something Steven wanted to explore.

Not all of Steven Spielberg's childhood was happy. Steven's family moved frequently, and his parents divorced. Some of his films feature a lonely or scared child seeking comfort or safety. Yet his films also express the joy and wonder of childhood. Like all great artists, Spielberg draws on his personal experiences. The grown man who made the movie called *E.T: The Extra-Terrestrial* was once a boy who missed his father and loved the mystery of outer space.

 **Write complete sentences to answer the question.**

Based on the article, what kind of person can you conclude Steven Spielberg is? How can you tell?

____

____

____

____

____

____

____

____

____

____

Name ______________________________ Date ____________

Comprehension and Vocabulary Review

Darken the circle by the best answer.

1. When Steven Spielberg was twelve, he _____.
   Ⓐ traveled in outer space
   Ⓑ charged admission to his homemade movies
   Ⓒ made the movie *Jaws*
   Ⓓ saw a movie about Davy Crockett

2. After Spielberg saw the movie about Davy Crockett, _____.
   Ⓐ he made his own movie about Davy Crockett
   Ⓑ he decided to become a pioneer
   Ⓒ he used some of Crockett's words as his motto
   Ⓓ he attacked a fort

3. What is the main idea of this article?
   Ⓐ Davy Crockett was a great hero.
   Ⓑ Steven Spielberg was a sad and lonely child.
   Ⓒ You should be a director like Steven Spielberg.
   Ⓓ Childhood was important to Steven Spielberg's career.

4. Which of these best explains what motivates Spielberg to be a success?
   Ⓐ He saw a movie about Davy Crockett when he was eight.
   Ⓑ He has made Oscar-winning movies.
   Ⓒ His motto is "Be sure you're right, then go ahead."
   Ⓓ He wanted to explore the mysteries of outer space.

5. A technique is _____.
   Ⓐ a spaceship
   Ⓑ a kind of meteor
   Ⓒ a kind of shark
   Ⓓ a way of doing something

6. Which fact would be least important to include in a summary?
   Ⓐ Young Steven was scared when his father wakened him to watch a meteor shower.
   Ⓑ Steven wanted to explore the mystery of outer space.
   Ⓒ Steven has directed films such as *E.T.* and *Jurassic Park.*
   Ⓓ Not all of Steven Spielberg's childhood was happy.

Write complete sentences to answer the questions.

7. What is the third paragraph mainly about?

____

____

8. What lesson can you learn from Steven Spielberg?

____

____

____

Name ______________________________ Date ____________

Japan: Industrial Leader of Asia

Japan is a crowded country with few natural resources. There is little farmland. Most people would expect Japan to be a poor country. But Japan is the richest country in Asia. It is Asia's industrial leader.

Japan's Landforms, Climate, and Resources

Japan is an **archipelago** country. It has four large islands. There are also thousands of small islands. Honshu is the largest island. Most Japanese people live on Honshu. Hills and mountains cover most of Japan. Thick forests cover Japan's mountains. About 60 of the mountains are volcanoes that sometimes erupt. Japan's tallest mountain is a beautiful volcano called Mount Fuji. Narrow coastal plains cover about one fifth of Japan. Most people live on these plains. Japan is a very crowded country because many people live on this small amount of land.

Japan has more earthquakes than any other nation. It has more than 1,000 earthquakes each year. Most of them are so small that no one feels them. But some cause great damage. In 1995 an earthquake in the city of Kobe killed more than 5,000 people.

The seas are important to Japan. The Sea of Japan is to the west of Japan. The Pacific Ocean is to the east. No place in the country is more than 100 miles from the sea. The Japanese use the seas for shipping and trading. Fishing is an important industry. The Japanese eat a lot of fish.

Japan's climate changes as you move from south to north. Islands in the south have hot summers and mild winters. The northern islands have cold winters and cool summers. But the island of Honshu has warm, humid summers and cold winters.

Japan has few resources. It gets wood from its forests. It creates some hydroelectric power from its rivers. Japan must import coal, oil, and raw materials.

Name ______________________ Date __________

People, Culture, and Government

About 126 million people live in Japan. They speak the Japanese language. They use thousands of characters to write their language. It is a difficult language to read. But everyone in Japan knows how to read and write. The Japanese people spend many years in school.

Many people in Japan practice both the Shinto and Buddhist religions. People who believe in the Shinto religion pray to many gods. These gods are found in rivers, mountains, trees, and other forms of nature. The country has thousands of Shinto and Buddhist temples.

Kimono

Japan is a very modern country, but the Japanese people love their old traditions. People bow to each other to say hello and goodbye. They show great respect for parents and for older people. They remove their shoes before they enter a home. They cover the floors of their homes with straw mats. People sometimes wear beautiful robes called **kimonos**. Some people enjoy planting small, beautiful gardens. They grow tiny trees called **bonsai** trees in flower pots.

The government of Japan is a democracy and a **constitutional monarchy**. It has a parliament and a prime minister. It also has an emperor. The emperor has no power in the government.

Japan: An Industrial Giant

Japan has a strong economy. Japan makes more factory products than all of the nations in Western Europe. In some years Japan produces more cars than the United States. The Japanese make excellent televisions, cars, cameras, computers, and other products. Their factories have the newest technology. Factories often use machines called robots to do many jobs.

Bonsai Tree

Trade has helped Japan become a rich country. Japan imports raw materials for its factories. It exports huge amounts of factory products. Japan limits the number of products it buys from the United States and other countries. So Japan has a favorable **balance of trade**. It exports much more than it imports.

About one third of the Japanese people work for large companies. These companies make their workers feel as if they are part of a large family. They treat their workers well. People work hard and receive good salaries. Many people work for one company until they are ready to retire.

Name ______________________ Date ____________

Farms, Cities, and Standard of Living

Japan has many mountains, so there is little farmland and most farms are small. Only a small part of the population works at farming. The Japanese are excellent farmers. They build **terraces** into the sides of hills so they can grow more crops. Terraces are large, flat areas of land for planting crops. The Japanese use fertilizers, good seeds, and modern machines. Farmers grow about two thirds of the food the country needs. Rice is the most important crop. Japan must import some of its food.

Japanese warships sailing past Mount Fuji

About three fourths of Japan's people live in cities. Most big cities are on the coast of the island of Honshu. Tokyo is Japan's capital and largest city. It is also a busy port. Tokyo is one of the largest cities in the world. It is also one of the most crowded. Most people travel around Tokyo by subway. Special city workers push people into the crowded trains so the doors will close. Tokyo is Japan's main business and arts center. It is also the home of the emperor's palace. People are allowed to visit the gardens around this famous palace.

Sapporo is the only large city on the northern island of Hokkaido. Every winter people visit Sapporo's ice festival. Visitors see temples, buildings, and statues that are carved out of ice. People can travel from Tokyo to Sapporo in very fast bullet trains. These trains go through a long tunnel that connects the islands of Honshu and Hokkaido.

Most people in Japan are part of the middle class. They have a good life. But Japan has two big problems. It is too crowded. There is a lot of pollution. Cars and factories are making the air and water dirty.

Look around your home. Look at the cars in the street. You will see many products from Japan. Japan is Asia's industrial leader.

Bullet Trains

Write About It

Write complete sentences to answer the question. Use another piece of paper if necessary.

Based on the article, why do you think Japan has become a rich industrial country?

____

____

____

Name ______________________________ Date ____________

Comprehension and Vocabulary Review

Use the words in the box to finish the paragraph below. Write the correct word on each line.

raw materials	**archipelago**	**pollution**	**forests**
constitutional monarchy	**Honshu**	**Tokyo**	

Japan is an ______________________ country with many islands. The largest island is ______________________. Most of Japan is covered with mountains and ______________________. Japan imports large amounts of ______________________ for its factories. Japan's government is a ______________________ because the emperor has no power. The emperor lives in ______________________, the country's capital. One of Japan's biggest problems is ______________________.

Darken the circle by the best answer.

1. Most Japanese people live on the island of _____.
   Ⓐ Asia
   Ⓑ Hokkaido
   Ⓒ Honshu
   Ⓓ Kobe
2. One of the main religions of Japan is _____.
   Ⓐ Bonsai
   Ⓑ Karate
   Ⓒ Christianity
   Ⓓ Shinto
3. Japanese robes are called _____.
   Ⓐ terraces
   Ⓑ kimonos
   Ⓒ bonsais
   Ⓓ robots
4. A small tree in a flower pot is a _____.
   Ⓐ Shinto
   Ⓑ terrace
   Ⓒ robot
   Ⓓ bonsai
5. Machines that are made to work like people are _____.
   Ⓐ subways
   Ⓑ robots
   Ⓒ exports
   Ⓓ terraces
6. Large, flat areas of land built into a mountain for growing crops are called _____.
   Ⓐ kimonos
   Ⓑ subways
   Ⓒ terraces
   Ⓓ imports

Name ______________________________ Date______________

Drawing Conclusions

Read each pair of sentences. Then look in the box for the conclusion you can make. Write the letter of the conclusion on the line.

a. The seas are important to Japan.
b. Japan does not have much farmland.
c. Japan has a favorable balance of trade.
d. Japanese factories have the newest technology.
e. Japan has few natural resources.
f. Traditions are important in Japan.

1. Most of Japan is covered with mountains.
There are narrow plains near the coast.

Conclusion ______

2. Japan has a large fishing industry.
Japan uses the seas for shipping and trading.

Conclusion ______

3. Japan must import all of its oil and coal.
Japan must import raw materials for industry.

Conclusion ______

4. The Japanese bow when they say hello and goodbye.
The Japanese remove their shoes before going into a home.

Conclusion ______

5. Japan exports more goods than it imports.
Japan limits the amount of goods it buys from other countries.

Conclusion ______

6. Japan manufactures many kinds of goods.
Factories often uses machines called robots to do many jobs.

Conclusion ______

LESSON 16

Fact or Opinion?

SELECTION DETAILS

Summary

"Fact or Opinion?" (page 105): The sample paragraphs give practice in identifying facts and opinions in short selections.

"Water on the Earth" (page 107): This article tells the importance of water and how it is often taken for granted.

Selection Type

Science Article

Comprehension Skill

Distinguish Fact from Opinion

Standards

Reading

- Distinguish fact from opinion in various texts.

Science

- Describe the role water plays on the Earth.

VOCABULARY

Introduce the vocabulary words. Write the words on the board. Help students find a definition for each word. Have students use each word in a sentence.

"Water on the Earth"
trillion

Tap Prior Knowledge

"Water on the Earth": Ask the students how much water they have used that day. Have them list the things they do with water. Is it important? Should it be taken for granted? Is it taken for granted?

Skill to Emphasize

Review the section about distinguishing facts and opinions on page 93. Tell the students to look for facts and opinions in the two articles. Facts can be proven, but opinions cannot be proven.

Preview Text Features

Have the students look for the opinions in the article. Opinions are beliefs, not facts. If the writer says water is taken for granted, he is expressing an opinion, not a fact. Boldfaced words indicate vocabulary words.

Comprehending the Selection

You may wish to model how to distinguish between facts and opinions by asking: *Which statements can be proved? Which statements cannot be proved?*

Reinforce the Comprehension Skill

Ask the students to identify some facts and opinions in the articles and explain how they decided which was which. Ask the students what the writer's purpose is in the article. Is the purpose personal, literary, persuasive, or informative? How is the purpose aided by the use of opinions in the selection? In the water article, the writer is trying to convince the reader that very important water is often taken for granted.

Distribute copies of the Fact-Opinion Chart on page 124 to help the students organize the information. Then have them complete the chart for the article.

Assess

Have the students complete the activities for the selection.

Distribute another Fact-Opinion Chart to the students. Have them use the chart to plan a letter on an issue they have opinions about. After they complete the chart, have them write a letter that contains both facts and opinions. Suggest that they send their letter to the editor of the local newspaper.

Name ______________________ Date ____________

Fact or Opinion?

A fact is a piece of information that can be proved true through observation or experimentation. An opinion is simply a person's belief or feeling about a topic.

Read each paragraph. Then darken the circle by the best answer for each question.

Television is more violent than ever. A recent national poll showed that 80% of adults think that there is too much violence on TV. Of these people, 59% say they are personally bothered by violent scenes. Yet, when students were polled, they didn't see anything wrong with the violence. Television networks are beginning to recognize the problem. They have been holding meetings to discuss how to reduce TV violence.

1. Which of the following is an opinion in the paragraph?
   Ⓐ Television is more violent than ever.
   Ⓑ Students don't see anything wrong.
   Ⓒ 59% of the people polled are bothered by violence.
   Ⓓ 80% of adults think there is too much violence on TV.

Today, with more than 20 million people, Mexico City is the largest metropolis in the world. Despite its modernization, the city's rich and colorful history is still alive. From its architecture to its culture and its food, many people agree that Mexico City is a fascinating city to visit.

2. Which of the following is a fact in the paragraph?
   Ⓐ Mexico City is fascinating.
   Ⓑ Mexico City has colorful food.
   Ⓒ Mexico City is the largest metropolis in the world.
   Ⓓ Mexico City is very modern.

The Oregon Trail was the land route used by many pioneers to settle the Pacific Northwest. The most common form of travel was by Conestoga wagon. Travel on the trail was dangerous. These brave pioneers had to cross swollen rivers and deal with disease, breakdowns, starvation, and lack of water. It was not uncommon to lose a quarter of the people from a wagon train before it reached its destination.

3. Which of the following is an opinion in the paragraph?
   Ⓐ The rivers were swollen.
   Ⓑ The pioneers were brave.
   Ⓒ There was disease.
   Ⓓ The wagons broke down.

Name ______________________ Date __________

Facts are used to inform, and opinions are used to persuade. Writers often use facts to support their opinions. They want to convince the reader that what they are claiming is true. If an article contains opinions, the writer is probably trying to persuade the reader.

Read each paragraph. Then write complete sentences to answer the questions.

The most persuasive voice for American independence belonged not to an American but to a British subject. Thomas Paine came to the colonies from England in 1774. An enemy of monarchy and of King George III, Paine wrote a pamphlet called *Common Sense*. In it he presented to the colonists arguments for independence. George Washington said that *Common Sense* contained "unanswerable reasoning." It was undoubtedly the chief cause of his decision to support American independence.

4. What are two facts you read in the paragraph? ______________________

____

5. What is an opinion you read in the paragraph? ______________________

____

6. What is the author's main idea in this paragraph? ______________________

____

Thomas Jefferson is considered to be America's chief Revolutionary hero. His political ideas in the *Declaration of Independence* laid the foundation for the new nation. Besides this accomplishment, he was an architect, a lawyer, an amateur musician and naturalist, and an inventor. Later, Thomas Jefferson served as President of the United States.

7. What are two facts you read in the paragraph? ______________________

____

8. What is an opinion you read in the paragraph? ______________________

____

9. What is the author's main idea in this paragraph? ______________________

____

Name ______________________________ Date ______________

Water on the Earth

Every day we take many things for granted. One thing we take for granted is water. No plant or animal could live without water. It is needed for drinking, cleaning, and keeping us cool. Our bodies are about two thirds water. We need about a quart of water a day to replace the water we lose naturally. All the food we eat and the things we use every day required much water in their making.

Americans use a half **trillion** gallons of water a day. Each person in the United States uses about 90 gallons of water a day for cleaning and gardening. Two more gallons per person are used for drinking and cooking. Factories use lots of water to make goods. It takes 60,000 gallons of water to make one ton of steel. Farmers use 115 gallons of water to grow the wheat for one loaf of bread, and 4,000 gallons are needed to get one pound of beef. As you can see, water is very important to us all. We must always be sure to take care of the water we have.

Darken the circle by the answer that best completes each sentence.

1. Water makes up about _____ of our bodies.
   Ⓐ one third
   Ⓑ one half
   Ⓒ two thirds
   Ⓓ None of the above

2. Americans use a _____ of water a day.
   Ⓐ half gallon
   Ⓑ half million gallons
   Ⓒ half trillion gallons
   Ⓓ None of the above

3. Which of these is a fact in the article?
   Ⓐ Every day we take many things for granted.
   Ⓑ One thing we take for granted is water.
   Ⓒ No plant or animal could live without water.
   Ⓓ As you can see, water is very important to us all.

4. Which of these is an opinion in the article?
   Ⓐ It takes 60,000 gallons of water to make one ton of steel.
   Ⓑ Farmers use 115 gallons of water to grow wheat for a loaf of bread.
   Ⓒ About 4,000 gallons are needed to get one pound of beef.
   Ⓓ We must always be sure to take care of the water we have.

Write a complete sentence to answer the question.

5. What is the author's main idea in this paragraph?

____

____

Purpose and Structure

SELECTION DETAILS

Summary
"Find the Purpose and Structure" (page 109): Gives practice in determining the writer's purpose and structure in short selections.

"Damascus" (page 110): Discusses the ancient city of Damascus.

"The Gettysburg Address" (page 111): Presents the original text of the Gettysburg Address as well as a paraphrased explanation of the speech.

"The Seven Wonders of the Modern World" (page 113): Classifies and describes seven wonderful structures of the modern world.

Selection Type
Social Studies Articles

Comprehension Skill
Draw Conclusions from Facts in a Nonfiction Article

Standards

Reading
- Make and explain inferences from texts such as drawing conclusions or determining purpose.

Social Studies
- Know adaptations that allow animals to survive
- Explain the significance of famous speeches to the duties of citizenship.
- Identify common characteristics of regions at local, national, and international scales on the basis of climate, landforms, ecosystems, and culture.

VOCABULARY

"Damascus"
inhabited, pharaohs, converted, cultural

"The Gettysburg Address"
conceived, proposition, dedicate, consecrate, hallow, detract, devotion, resolve

"The Seven Wonders of the Modern World"
renowned, compile, span, symmetrical, heralded, memorial, mausoleum, spires

Tap Prior Knowledge

"Damascus": Ask the students if they know any of the famous cities of the ancient world. What do they know about these places?

"The Gettysburg Address": Ask the students if they know about Lincoln's Gettysburg Address. Why did he make the speech?

"The Seven Wonders of the Modern World": Ask the students what they think would make something a wonder of the world. What wonders would they choose?

Skill to Emphasize

Review the section about purpose and structure on page 93. The reader at times must identify the writer's purpose for writing. The reader must also at times identify the organizational structures the writer has used. A student is best able to analyze a writing through the writer's purpose and structure.

Preview Text Features

Have the students look at the original speech and the explanation in "The Gettysburg Address." The explanation gives a simplified version of the speech. Point out the map in "The Seven Wonders of the Modern World." It shows the locations of the wonders discussed in the article. The illustrations in this article give the students a better idea of the wonders. Boldfaced words indicate vocabulary words.

Comprehending the Selection

Model a better understanding of conclusion by asking: *Using the facts given, what conclusions can you make about the the writer's purpose and structure?*

Reinforce the Comprehension Skill

Tell the students that a good conclusion is based on all the facts of the article. They should be sure their conclusions make sense and include all the facts. The students first need to decide on the main idea of the article. If they can determine the main idea, they can usually determine the writer's purpose. The writer achieves purpose through structure.

Assess

Have the students complete the activities for the selection.

Have the students write a speech about a topic they find important in today's world.

Name ______________________ Date ____________

Find the Purpose and Structure

Readers must sometimes determine a writer's purpose for writing. Personal writing tells something about the writer or how the writer feels about something. Literary writing tells a story or a poem. Persuasive writing tries to make the readers change their minds about some issue. Informative writing tells facts about a topic. The reader must decide which of these purposes the writer has used. The reader should also be able to recognize the organizational structure of the writing.

Read each paragraph. Then darken the circle by the best answer for each question.

Most states now have recycling programs. However, they all need to expand what is being recycled. Most towns recycle cans, glass, paper, cardboard, and magazines. Yet we still buy many items made of plastic and foam. Currently only about 5% of these materials are recycled. If we want to reduce the amount of garbage we throw away, we must make changes in the way we do recycling.

1. What purpose do you think the writer used to write this paragraph?
   Ⓐ personal Ⓒ persuasive
   Ⓑ literary Ⓓ informative

The Moon is smaller than Earth. It is about 238,000 miles away from Earth. The Moon has no air or water. During the day, the Moon is unbearably hot. At night it is colder than the North Pole. The Moon is covered with dusty, flat land and has many craters. On July 20, 1969, Neil Armstrong made history by being the first man to walk on the Moon. He had to wear a special space suit to protect himself from the Moon's environment. Armstrong and other astronauts helped us learn a lot about the Moon.

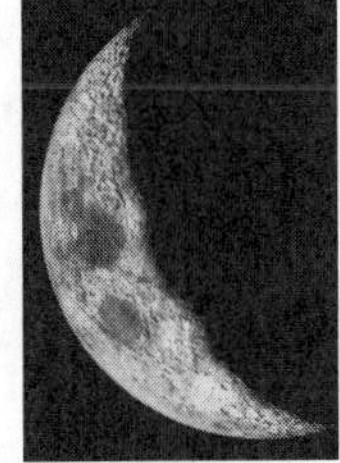

2. What purpose do you think the writer used to write this paragraph?
   Ⓐ personal Ⓒ persuasive
   Ⓑ literary Ⓓ informative

Nonfiction is a form of literature that includes many types of writing. Some of these types are essays, biographies, and articles. The basic difference between fiction and nonfiction is that nonfiction is concerned with true facts, ideas, and events.

3. What purpose do you think the writer used to write this paragraph?
   Ⓐ personal Ⓒ persuasive
   Ⓑ literary Ⓓ informative

4. Which of these organizational structures did the writer use in this paragraph?
   Ⓐ narration of event
   Ⓑ cause-effect
   Ⓒ classification
   Ⓓ narration of process

I think that some students are so afraid that they will fail a test that they panic. Their minds go totally blank. Then they feel that they have to cheat in order to pass. Personally, I like to take tests, and I would never cheat.

5. What purpose do you think the writer used to write this paragraph?
   Ⓐ personal Ⓒ persuasive
   Ⓑ literary Ⓓ informative

Name ______________________ Date ____________

Damascus

Damascus is believed to be the oldest continuously **inhabited** city in the world. Damascus was first inhabited 7,000 years ago. It was known to the Egyptian **pharaohs** and is mentioned in the Book of Genesis in the *Bible*.

The main attraction in the old city is the Souk al-Hamidiya, the marketplace where vendors call to shoppers to come see what they are selling. They usually say, "Come see, no charge for looking." The tiny stores overflow with silk and inlaid wood boxes made in Syria, spices from India and Africa, carpets from Iran, and brass pots from Central Asia.

Hidden behind wooden doors along the winding, twisting lanes are Ottoman-era palaces, rich with hand-carved wood, marble, and decorative stone inlays. Some of these palaces are private homes, but many are being **converted** for other uses, such as a Danish **cultural** center and a hands-on laboratory for University of Damascus architecture students.

 **Darken the circle by the best answer for each question.**

1. Why do people believe that Damascus is the oldest city in the world?
   Ⓐ The Souk in the Old City has many vendors.
   Ⓑ Ottoman-era palaces are still being used.
   Ⓒ Egyptian pharaohs knew about it, and it is mentioned in the *Bible*.
   Ⓓ There is a hands-on laboratory for University of Damascus architecture students.

2. What does the word *converted* mean in this selection?
   Ⓐ persuaded
   Ⓑ changed
   Ⓒ retained
   Ⓓ maintained

3. Which statement about Damascus is not true?
   Ⓐ It is about 7,000 years old.
   Ⓑ You can buy things from many countries.
   Ⓒ All the old palaces are private homes.
   Ⓓ Egyptian pharaohs knew about the city.

4. What will the architecture students probably study?
   Ⓐ how the old palaces were built
   Ⓑ how to make the stores larger
   Ⓒ where to buy carpets from Iran
   Ⓓ how to carve wood

5. Why do you think the author wrote this article?
   Ⓐ to tell you where to buy Indian spices
   Ⓑ to tell you about Egyptian pharaohs
   Ⓒ to tell you about the Danish cultural center
   Ⓓ to tell you about the city of Damascus

6. What purpose do you think the writer used to write this article?
   Ⓐ personal
   Ⓑ literary
   Ⓒ persuasive
   Ⓓ informative

Name ______________________________ Date ____________

The Gettysburg Address

One of the great battles of the Civil War was fought at Gettysburg, Pennsylvania, in early July 1863. Over 50,000 Union and Confederate soldiers died in the battle. A military cemetery was built at Gettysburg for the thousands of Union soldiers who died there. The dedication of the cemetery took place on November 19, 1863. President Lincoln was asked to give a short speech since he was not the main speaker that day. In his speech Lincoln told Americans that the purpose of the Civil War was to make the United States a democracy with freedom and liberty for all. The Gettysburg Address lasted only two minutes, but today it is considered one of the nation's greatest speeches.

The original speech is followed by an explanation. What is Lincoln's purpose in giving the speech?

> Four score and seven years ago our fathers brought forth on this continent, a new nation, **conceived** in Liberty, and dedicated to the **proposition** that all men are created equal.
>
> Now we are engaged in a great civil war, testing whether that nation, or any nation so conceived and so dedicated, can long endure. We are met on a great battlefield of that war. We have come to **dedicate** a portion of that field, as a final resting place for those who here gave their lives that that nation might live. It is altogether fitting and proper that we should do this.
>
> But, in a larger sense, we can not dedicate—we can not **consecrate**—we can not **hallow**—this ground. The brave men, living and dead, who struggled here, have consecrated it, far above our poor power to add or **detract**. The world will little note, nor long remember what we say here, but it can never forget what they did here. It is for us the living, rather, to be dedicated here to the unfinished work which they who fought here have thus far so nobly advanced. It is rather for us to be here dedicated to the great task remaining before us—that from these honored dead we take increased **devotion** to that cause for which they gave the last full measure of devotion—that we here highly **resolve** that these dead shall not have died in vain—that this nation, under God, shall have a new birth of freedom—and that government of the people, by the people, for the people, shall not perish from the earth.

Explanation of the Gettysburg Address

Paragraph 1: Eighty-seven years ago, in 1776, our leaders created a new nation based on the idea of liberty. The United States would exist to prove the statement that "all men are created equal."

Paragraph 2: Now we are fighting a civil war. This war is a test to see if the United States, or any other nation, can exist for a long time if it is based on the ideas of liberty and equality. We are now meeting at the battlefield of Gettysburg. We have come to dedicate part of the battlefield as a cemetery for soldiers who died here. Those soldiers died fighting so that the United States would continue to be a nation based on ideas of liberty and equality. It is correct and proper that we dedicate this cemetery to honor those dead soldiers.

Name ______________________________ Date____________

Paragraph 3: But we really do not have the power to dedicate this cemetery and make this ground holy. We cannot do this because this cemetery has already been made holy by the brave men, living and dead, who fought at Gettysburg. We cannot do anything more to make this cemetery holy than they have already done. The world will not notice or remember what we say here today. But the world can never forget what they did at Gettysburg. It must be our job to dedicate our own lives to the work these soldiers fought for so hard but could not finish. We must dedicate ourselves to the great cause for which these soldiers died. To honor them, we must work harder than ever for this cause. We must prove that these soldiers did not die without a reason. We must work hard so that this nation, under God, will have a government that allows equality and liberty for all people. We must make sure that this democratic government will never be destroyed.

Darken the circle by the best answer.

1. Why did people gather at Gettysburg on November 19, 1863?
   Ⓐ to fight
   Ⓑ to build a cemetery
   Ⓒ to dedicate a cemetery
   Ⓓ to put up mailboxes

2. A proposition is _____.
   Ⓐ a part of an airplane
   Ⓑ an idea offered for acceptance
   Ⓒ a burial place
   Ⓓ a mistake

3. In Lincoln's speech, *to resolve* means to _____.
   Ⓐ solve again
   Ⓑ shout
   Ⓒ make a firm decision
   Ⓓ wonder about

4. What purpose do you think Lincoln used to write this speech?
   Ⓐ personal
   Ⓑ literary
   Ⓒ persuasive
   Ⓓ informative

Write complete sentences to answer the questions. Use a separate piece of paper to write your answers.

5. Why do you think Lincoln wrote this speech?

6. Why did Lincoln say "we can not dedicate—we can not consecrate—we can not hallow this ground?"

7. How does Lincoln think Americans should finish the work for which the Union soldiers fought?

Name ________________________________ Date____________

The Seven Wonders of the Modern World

The ancient Greeks and Romans made many different lists of man-made wonders of the world. Buildings and statues would qualify for the lists based on their size or another unusual quality. The most **renowned** list is now called the Seven Wonders of the Ancient World. All of those wonders were located in a small region around the Mediterranean Sea.

Today, many more amazing man-made wonders have been constructed all over the world. In the tradition of the Greeks and Romans, we can **compile** our own list of wonders that **span** the globe. These are wonders that we can visit today. Only one of the original seven ancient wonders still exists. A tour of today's wonders starts there, in the deserts of Egypt.

The Great Pyramid of Giza

The pyramids of Egypt were tombs for pharaohs. The largest pyramid was built at Giza, for Pharaoh Kuhfu. When it was completed in 2580 B.C., it was the tallest structure in the world. It held that record for nearly 4,000 years. It is made up of over two million blocks of heavy limestone and granite. How did the ancient Egyptians build this massive structure without machines? No one knows for sure. However, most experts think the blocks were hauled up sloping ramps with ropes. Visitors from all over the world still flock to see this ancient wonder today.

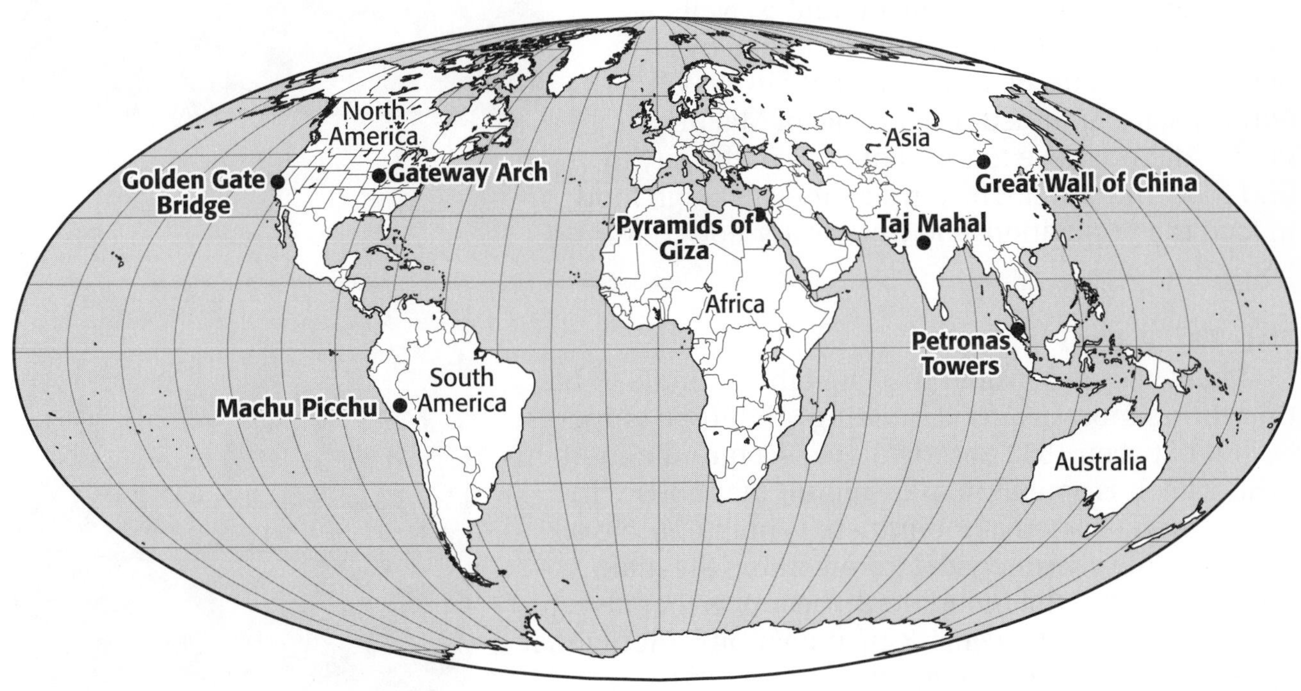

Name ________________________________ Date ____________

The Great Wall of China

The Great Wall of China snakes through the mountains of northern China for more than 1,500 miles (2,414 kilometers). If it were in the U.S., it would stretch from Washington, D.C., to Denver, Colorado. The Great Wall is so large that it can even be seen from space.

The Great Wall started in different places as protection for different states. The individual sections were connected during the Qin (CHIN) Dynasty from 221–206 B.C. This tradition of connecting the wall lasted for centuries. Each dynasty added to the wall's height, length, and design.

During the Ming dynasty, from 1368–1644 A.D., the wall took on its present form. The brick work was enlarged, and sophisticated designs were added. Many parts of the wall have been destroyed over the years. However, much of the wall has been restored, so visitors can still see this achievement.

Machu Picchu

Machu Picchu (MAH choo PEEK choo) is the site of an ancient Inca city located in Peru on a mountain top. This ancient city is hidden between two larger peaks. Built between 1460 and 1470 A.D., Machu Picchu was remarkably intact when it was discovered in 1911 by an American explorer. This ancient city consists of stone buildings, walls, towers, and terraces. Everything is linked by a network of 3,000 steps. This ancient city was entirely self-contained. The people of Machu Picchu did not have to travel outside of the city to find food and water. The terraces grew enough food to feed the population, and fresh water flowed from natural springs.

The Taj Mahal

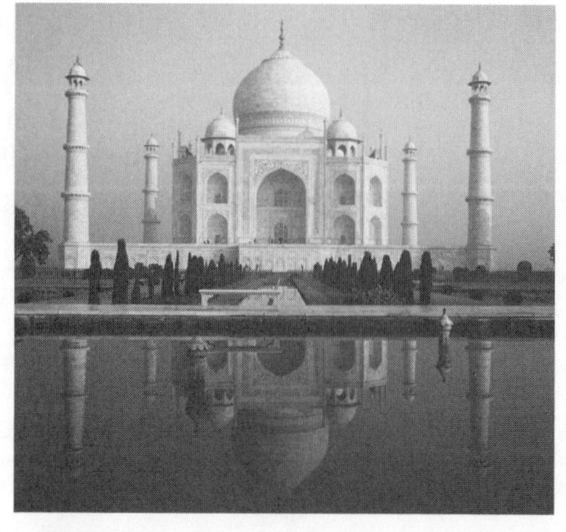

Many people consider the Taj Mahal in India to be the world's most beautiful building. An Indian emperor built it between 1632 and 1648 A.D. as a monument to his dead wife. It is actually a **mausoleum** that houses her grave. This spectacular monument is built entirely of white marble. **Symmetrical** towers frame the main building. Part of the monument's beauty is that it seems to change color. At dawn, it can appear pink. At night, it seems to glow in the moonlight.

Name ______________________ Date __________

The Golden Gate Bridge

The Golden Gate Bridge, located in San Francisco, California, has been **heralded** as one of the top construction achievements of the twentieth century. The height of the towers reaches 746 feet (227 meters) above the water of the Golden Gate Strait. The total length of the bridge spans 8,981 feet (2,737 meters). The Golden Gate Bridge is known as one of the world's most beautiful bridges. It has tremendous towers, sweeping cables, and brilliant color. The bridge was ready for cars in 1938.

The Gateway Arch

Soaring 630 feet (192 meters) above the Mississippi River, the Gateway Arch in Saint Louis, Missouri, is America's tallest human-made monument. The Gateway Arch is a **memorial** to Thomas Jefferson and to the historic role Saint Louis played as the gateway to the west. The construction of this astounding stainless steel arch was completed in 1965.

Petronas Twin Towers

Until 1998, the world's tallest skyscraper had always been in the United States. But that year, the Petronas Twin Towers in Kuala Lumpur, Malaysia, squeaked past Chicago's Sears Tower by 33 feet (10 meters). The **spires** on top of the Petronas Towers peak at an impressive 1,483 feet (452 meters). The identical towers are linked by a bridge which creates a dramatic gateway to Kuala Lumpur. Other features of these towers include a curtain wall of glass and stainless steel sun shades. The shades are important because Malaysia is close to the equator where the Sun's rays are the strongest.

Name ______________________ Date ____________

Comprehension Review

Darken the circle by the best answer.

1. What purpose do you think the writer used to write this article?
   - Ⓐ personal
   - Ⓑ literary
   - Ⓒ persuasive
   - Ⓓ informative

2. What is the main organizational pattern the author used to write this article?
   - Ⓐ narration of event
   - Ⓑ cause-effect
   - Ⓒ classification
   - Ⓓ comparison-contrast

Write complete sentences to answer each question.

3. Why do you think the author selected these particular structures to write about?

____

____

4. How are the Pyramid at Giza and the Taj Mahal alike? How are they different?

____

____

____

5. What are some descriptive details used by the author to tell about the Petronas Twin Towers?

____

____

6. Why was the Great Wall of China built?

____

____

7. Why was the Gateway Arch built?

____

____

8. Which of these wonders would you most like to visit? Tell why.

____

____

____

____

____

Name ______________________________ Date ____________

Vocabulary Review

Darken the circle by the best answer.

1. In this article, *compile* means _____.
   Ⓐ put together
   Ⓑ take apart
   Ⓒ take down
   Ⓓ put away

2. In this article, *span* means _____.
   Ⓐ far away
   Ⓑ leave behind
   Ⓒ bring together
   Ⓓ stretch across

3. In this article, *sophisticated* means _____.
   Ⓐ simply designed; plain
   Ⓑ cleverly designed; complicated
   Ⓒ incredibly large; massive
   Ⓓ extremely ugly; offensive

4. In this article, *heralded* means _____.
   Ⓐ listened; heard
   Ⓑ scolded; warned
   Ⓒ proclaimed; announced
   Ⓓ wished; hoped

5. In this article, *spires* means _____.
   Ⓐ bridges that span long distances
   Ⓑ monuments to honor royalty
   Ⓒ structures that come to a point
   Ⓓ tombs that house ancient rulers

6. In this article, *memorial* means _____.
   Ⓐ a fond recollection
   Ⓑ a monument to honor a dead person
   Ⓒ a large gate
   Ⓓ bigger than anything else

Build Your Vocabulary

Analogies are pairs of words that have the same relationship.

Complete each analogy with a word from the box.

mausoleum	**pharaohs**	**renowned**	**symmetrical**

7. *United States* is to *presidents* as *Ancient Egypt* is to ______________________.
8. *Unpopular* is to *popular* as *unknown* is to ______________________.
9. *Book* is to *library* as *tomb* is to ______________________.
10. *Unbalanced* is to *balanced* as *uneven* is to ______________________.

Name ______________________ Date ______________

Main Idea Map

Details

Main Idea

Details

Main Idea

Name ______________________________ Date ______________

Summary Chart

Important Idea

____

____

____

____

Important Idea

____

____

____

____

Important Idea

____

____

____

____

Summary

____

____

____

____

____

____

____

____

____

____

____

____

____

____

Name ______________________ Date ____________

Sequence Chart

Event 1

Event 2

Event 3

Event 4

Sequence Chart

Event 1

Event 2

Event 3

Event 4

Name ________________________ Date ____________

Cause-Effect Charts

Cause

Effect

Cause

Effect

Effect 1

Cause

Effect 2

Effect 3

Name ______________________ Date ____________

Classification Tree Diagram

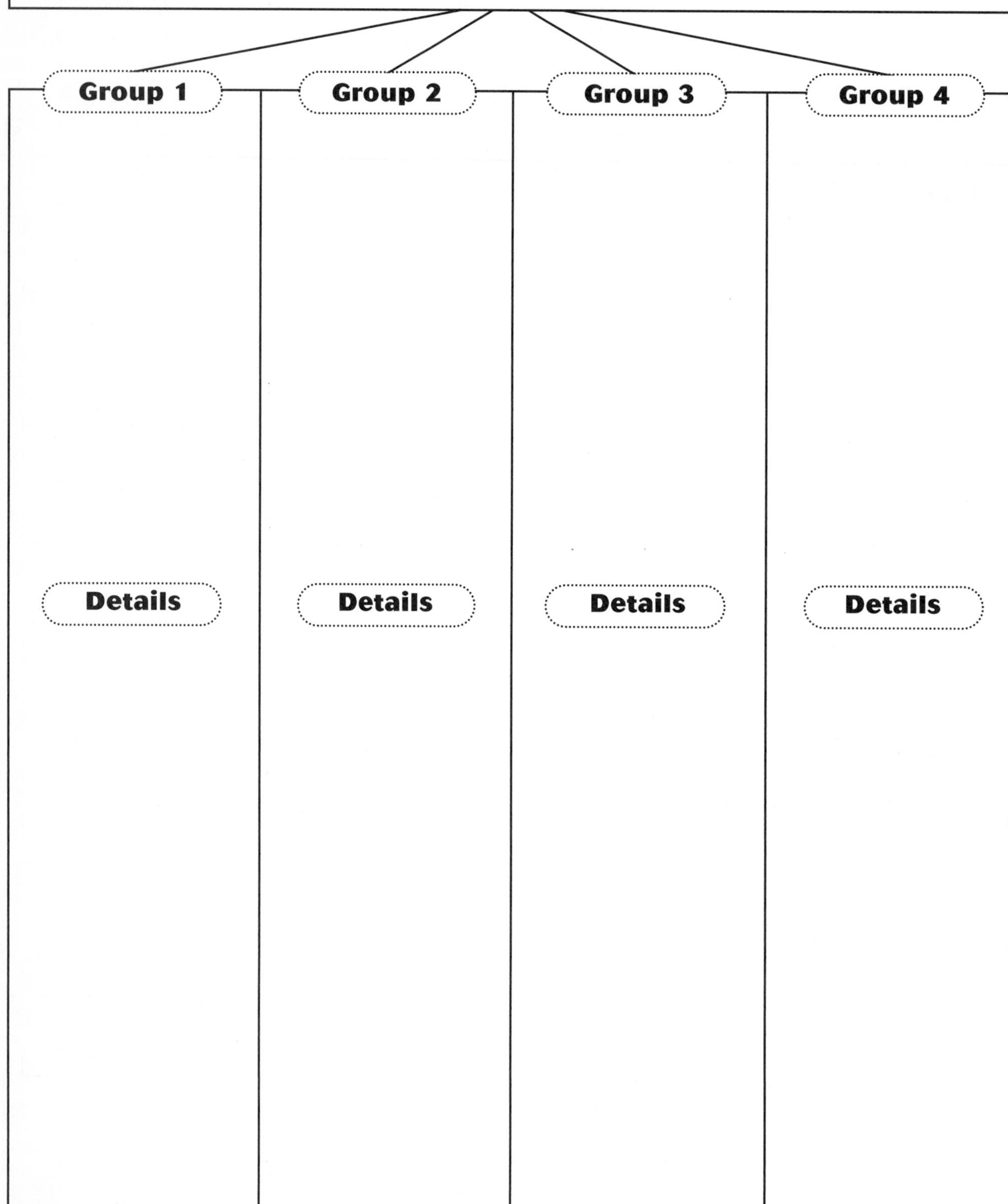

Name ______________________________ Date ______________

Venn Diagram

Main similarities:

____

____

Main differences:

____

____

Name ______________________ Date __________

Fact-Opinion Chart

Sentence	Fact or Opinion?	How I Know
1.		
2.		
3.		
4.		

Nonfiction Comprehension

Reading Strategies for the Content Areas

Middle School

Answer Key

Page 8

1. C
2. B
3. A
4. D

Sentences will vary.

5. Three diseases caused by viruses are colds, flu, and measles.
6. A virus causes disease by getting inside a body cell and changing the way the cell works.
7. After taking over a body cell, the virus reproduces inside the cell; then the cell bursts open and the virus particles spread to other cells.
8. Measles can be spread by breathing the air around an infected person or using an infected person's towel or dishes.

Page 10

1. A
2. D
3. A
4. B
5. A
6. C

Sentences will vary.

7. There are fewer animals in the higher trophic levels because each animal needs more food to stay alive.
8. In a food web with many levels, the creatures at the highest levels would have very little food to eat and would be more likely to die.

Page 12

Sentences will vary.

1. The United States produced about 7 million barrels of oil per day in 1960.
2. The United States produced just over 7 million barrels of oil per day in 1990.
3. Though oil production peaked in the mid-1970s and mid-1980s, the oil production in 1960 and 1990 was about the same.
4. The United States used about 10 million barrels of oil per day in 1960.
5. The United States used about 17 million barrels of oil per day in 1990.
6. Oil usage in the United States increased steadily from 1960 to 1980, then leveled off.
7. Oil production and usage were not in balance between 1960 and 1990. The United States uses much more oil than it produces.

Page 13

1. B
2. A
3. B
4. A
5. D
6. B
7. B
8. D
9. Answers will vary. Possible response: Cheyenne has a fairly dry climate.

Page 15

1. Boston, Massachusetts, has the highest average tidal range.
2. Portland, Maine, has a higher average tidal range than Seattle, Washington.
3. Key West, Galveston, and Honolulu have the same average tidal range.
4. The average tidal range in Savannah, Georgia, is 2.2 meters.
5. The difference between the highest average tidal range and the lowest average tidal range is 2.5 meters.

Page 16

1. 785
2. Chart:

Dumb Dog: Week One—Rating, 15.9, Share 33; Week Two—Rating, 14.7, Share 33; Week Three—Rating, 14.7, Share 30
Time Warp: Week One—Rating, 20.1, Share 42; Week Two—Rating, 15.6, Share 35; Week Two—Rating, 19.6, Share 40
Winnie's Wanders: Week One—Rating, 12.4, Share 26; Week Two—Rating, 14.1, Share 32; Week Three—Rating, 15.1, Share 31

3. There were different numbers of households watching TV.
4. *Winnie's Wanders*

Page 17

1. $37.50
2. $42.25
3. Toxaco
4. Toxaco
5. $0.46
6. $3,200.00
7. 17

Page 18

1. C
2. D
3. B
4. C

Page 20

1. Khartoum
2. Red Sea
3. Kuwait City; about 400 miles
4. about 600 kilometers
5. Tigris River and Euphrates River
6. Syria, Turkey, Iraq, and Iran

Page 21

1. The red bat migrates between the coniferous forest and the deciduous forest biomes.
2. The monarch butterfly has more than one migratory route.
3. The red bat and the myrtle warbler migrate between the same two biomes.
4. The myrtle warbler spends the winter in the deciduous forest biome.
5. Answers will vary.

Page 22

1. D
2. B
3. C
4. D
5. Texas probably has the most agricultural activity because it has more plains.

Pages 25–26

1. D
2. B
3. D
4. A
5. C
6. A
7. C
8. B

Page 28

1. C
2. C
3. A
4. B
5. D
6. B
7. A
8. C
9. Answers will vary.

Page 32

1. C
2. B
3. C
4. B
5. C
6. A
7. One type of surfer participates in organized competitions, and the second type of surfer enjoys surfing in private for the personal pleasure it gives.
8. Since the 15th century, surfing has increased in popularity, and now surfers have their own identity. Surfboards have also changed in size, shape, and weight.

Page 33
1. envelop
2. eliminate
3. transformed
4. circuit
5. cresting; a
6. precise; b
7. maneuver; b
8. prolonging; a
9. array; a
10. identity; a

Page 35
1. C
2. B
3. C
4. C
5. C

Page 36
1. B
2. D
3. B
4. C

Page 37
1. D
2. B
3. A solar eclipse is an eclipse of the Sun.
4. A solar eclipse is caused when the Moon passes between the Sun and Earth, and the shadow of the Moon falls on Earth.

Page 38
1. 120 without milk; 190 with milk
2. carbohydrates
3. sugar
4. Recommended Daily Allowance
5. 25%
6. Vitamins A, D, B4, B12
7. wheat bran, raisins, sugar, salt, malt flavoring (Ingredients are listed in order of amounts.)
8. increase protein by adding whole milk

Page 40
Main ideas may vary.
Paragraph 1: The oceans cover about two thirds of the Earth's surface.
Paragraph 2: Over nine tenths of the Earth's water is salty.
Paragraph 3: The ocean floor contains many of the same landform features found on the continents.
Paragraph 4: Measuring the depths of the oceans is not easy.
Paragraph 5: As the depth of the ocean water increase, its pressure also increases.
Summaries will vary. Sample summary: The oceans cover about two thirds of the Earth's surface and contain about nine tenths of the Earth's water. The ocean floor has landform features similar to the continents. Measuring the depth of the ocean waters is not easy because as the depth increases, the pressure increases, so humans need special precautions in the depths of the oceans.

Page 41
Major ideas and details will vary but should reflect the content of the article.

Page 42
1. C
2. D
3. B
4. D
5. A
6. C

Summaries will vary. Sample response: The Inuit people live in the Arctic regions of the world. For centuries, the Inuit hunted whale, walrus, reindeer, and seal, but these times have passed, and today most Inuit use modern conveniences. Some Inuit, though, are fighting to keep the traditional ways of life alive.

Page 43
Major ideas and details will vary but should reflect the content of the article.

Page 44
1. D
2. B
3. D
4. B
5. A
6. C

Summaries will vary. Sample response: After World War II, fear of Communism was strong in the United States. Many people in government were accused of being Communists. One notable person was Alger Hiss, who appeared before the House Committee on Un-American Activities. Hiss said he that he was not a Communist. He was not proved to be a Communist, but he was found guilty of lying. Senator Joseph McCarthy was the main person accusing people of being Communists. He never proved anyone guilty, but he ruined many people's careers. McCarthy lost power when other Senators stood up against him and he also charged that the army was full of Communists.

Page 47
1. C
2. D
3. B
4. C

Page 48
1. C
2. B
3. A
4. A

Page 49
Answers will vary.
1913: Jesse Owens was born.
1921: Jesse's family moved to Ohio.
1935 Owens broke four track records for running and jumping. He was chosen to represent the United States in the 1936 Olympic Games.
1936: Owens won four gold medals at the Olympic Games. Adolf Hitler refused to award Owens his medals.
1980: Jesse Owens died.

Page 50
1. C
2. D
3. B
4. D
5. A
6. B
7. C
8. B

Answers will vary on Hitler's response.

Page 52
Sentences will vary but should include key events at each date or time.
August 28: The women began climbing the mountain.
October 13: The team reached the 24,200-foot mark and set up camp.
October 15, 3:00 A.M.: First group awoke; Kramer dropped out because of frostbite.
October 15, 7:00 A.M.: The others in the group began the climb to the summit.
October 15, 3:30 P.M.: The group reached the summit.
October 17: Second team began climb to summit, but guide got sick and turned back.
October 19: Women in second team had disappeared and were found dead.

Page 53
1. C
2. B
3. D
4. C
5. B
6. A
7. B
8. D
9. Answers will vary. The story says that Blum used a tape recorder, so her dialogue is more likely factual.

Page 55
Chart: Mercury, 14 kg; Venus, 42.5 kg; Jupiter, 130 kg; Saturn, 60 kg; Uranus, 55 kg; Neptune, 70 kg
1. Mercury
2. Jupiter
3. Jupiter, Saturn, Uranus, Neptune
4. Mercury, Venus, Mars
5. 4.25 pounds
6. 5.6 pounds

Page 56
1. B
2. D

Sentences will vary.

3. Water rushing from Lake Erie to Lake Ontario carved out the Niagara River and then passed over a steep cliff, creating the falls.
4. First, water from the river above the falls is diverted into underground pipes. The water travels through the pipes and passes through turbines as it is returned to the river below the falls. The turbines power generators that produce electricity.

Page 57
Order: 4, 5, 2, 1, 3

Page 58
1. B
2. C
3. D
4. B
5. A
6. D

Sentences will vary.

7. After the supernova forms, the amount of material that remains after the explosion will determine if the star will be a neutron star or a black hole.
8. Explanations will vary but should indicate that the Sun is the star stage of its life cycle.

Pages 60–61
1. B
2. C
3. B
4. C
5. B
6. C
7. C
8. B

Page 62
1. C
2. D
3. B
4. C

Sentences will vary.

5. First, farmers planted wheat, which destroyed the prairie grasses that had the soil in place. Then, seven years of drought left the soil dry and loose. Wind storms blew dust off the dry fields, and everything in the area was coated with dust.
6. To prevent another Dust Bowl, people have planted thousands of trees to hold down the soil and block the wind on the Great Plains.

Page 67
1. D
2. B
3. C
4. D

Sentences will vary.

5. Causes will vary but should include some of the causes listed on pages 64 through 66.
6. The effect of the declaration was the American Revolution and eventual independence.

Page 68
1. B
2. C
3. D
4. B
5. A
6. D
7. A
8. D

Vocabulary choices and sentences will vary.

Page 71
1. D
2. B
3. B
4. C
5. Shipping the blossoms can cause bruising, which causes the blossoms to turn brown.

Page 73
1. B
2. D
3. C
4. B
5. A
6. C
7. B
8. C
9. Answers will vary but should include a mention of length, color, or shape of snouts and teeth.

Page 75
The three parts of an atom are the proton, neutron, and electron.

Page 76
1. Atoms are made of protons, neutrons, and electrons.
2. Electrons have a negative electric charge.
3. Neutrons have no electric charge.
4. Protons have a positive electric charge.
5. The nucleus is made of protons and neutrons.
6. B
7. A
8. B
9. A
10. B
11. D
12. D

Page 78
The four parts of the business cycle are expansion, peak, recession, and trough.

Page 79
1. B
2. B
3. A
4. C
5. A
6. B

Summaries will vary. Check that responses contain at least six of the words or phrases in the box.

Page 82
1. B
2. A
3. C
4. A
5. The three kinds of rocks are igneous, sedimentary, and metamorphic.

Page 84
1. B
2. C
3. D
4. A
5. The effects caused by poisonous plants are the effect on the skin of people who touch the plant and the harmful effect to people if they eat the plant.
6. Answers will vary but should suggest that being poisonous is a protective adaptation.
7. Answers will vary but should include two of these three: poison ivy, poison oak, poison sumac.
8. Answers will vary but should include one of these plants: wild mushrooms, lily-of-the-valley, daffodil, azalea, rhubarb leaves.

Page 86
The four economic systems discussed in the article are the traditional economy, the command economy, the market economy, and the mixed economy.

Page 87
1. B
2. A
3. C
4. B
5. D
6. D

Paragraphs will vary but should include four or more of the phrases or words in the box. In addition, the paragraph should point out that command economies are controlled by the government and market economies are controlled by the people.

Page 89
1. A ground squirrel's heart beats 2 to 10 times per minute during hibernation.
2. A brown bat's heart beats 400 to 700 times per minute when it is awake.
3. The ground squirrel and the hamster have the same heartbeat rate when they are awake.
4. The woodchuck's body temperature remains highest during hibernation.

Page 90
1. An air mass has about the same temperature, pressure, and humidity throughout.
2. An air mass over land will be drier.
3. A warm front, a cold front, or a stationary front can form between air masses.
4. A cold air mass has colder air and usually includes thunderstorms with much precipitation. A warm air mass has warmer air; storms may occur along a warm front, but the precipitation is usually not as heavy as along a cold front.

Page 91
1. Sun Kachina is a spirit of nature.
2. The kachinas wear different masks or face painting and different clothing. They also act differently.
3. The headdress represents the Sun because the feathers spread out like the Sun's rays.
4. Answers will vary. Accept reasonable responses with appropriate explanations.

Page 92
1. D
2. C
3. G
4. B
5. E
6. A
7. F

Page 94
1. C
2. A
3. C
4. A
5. Answers will vary. Possible response: The main difference between a series circuit and a parallel circuit is that power is delivered differently to the devices in the circuit.
6. Answers will vary. Possible response: In a series circuit, all the lights would go out, so each bulb would have to be checked separately to see if it still works.

Pages 95–96
1. C
2. D
3. B
4. B
5. D

Acceptable conclusions: a, b, d

Page 97
Answers will vary.

Page 98
1. B
2. C
3. D
4. C
5. D
6. A
7. The third paragraph is about young Steven being taken to see a meteor shower by his father.
8. Answers will vary but might suggest that you should know that what you are doing is right, then go ahead.

Page 99
Answers will vary but might suggest that Japan uses new technology, maintains a good company-worker relationship, and has a favorable balance of trade.

Page 102
Paragraph answers in order: archipelago, Honshu, forests, raw materials, constitutional monarchy, Tokyo, pollution
1. C
2. D
3. B
4. D
5. B
6. C

Page 103
1. b
2. a
3. e
4. f
5. c
6. d

Pages 105–106
1. A
2. C
3. B

Answers will vary. Possible responses are given.

4. Thomas Paine came to America in 1774. He wrote *Common Sense*, which presented arguments for colonial independence.
5. Thomas Paine was the most persuasive voice for American independence.
6. The British citizen Thomas Paine was a more important voice for American independence than any American voice.
7. Jefferson was an architect and a lawyer. He was President of the United States.
8. Jefferson is considered to be America's chief Revolutionary hero.
9. Thomas Jefferson was a remarkable man.

Page 107
1. C
2. C
3. C
4. D
5. The author's main idea is that water is our most important resource, but too many people take it for granted.

Page 109
1. C
2. D
3. D
4. C
5. A

Page 110
1. C
2. B
3. C
4. A
5. D
6. D

Page 112
1. C
2. B
3. C
4. C

Answers will vary. Possible responses are given.

5. Lincoln wrote this speech to convince the people in the North to continue fighting the Civil War.
6. He believed that the men who had fought and died for a noble cause had already dedicated the ground and made it holy.
7. Lincoln believes that his listeners must make a renewed effort to preserve the United States of America and its form of government.

Page 116
1. D
2. C

Answers will vary. Possible responses are given.

3. All of the wonders listed in the article are impressive for unique reasons. These wonders can all be visited today.
4. Both buildings are monuments to the dead and are made of stone. They are different in both shape and location.
5. The towers are 1,483 feet tall, they have spires, and they are linked by a bridge. The towers have a curtain wall of glass and stainless steel sun shades.
6. The Great Wall was originally built to provide protection for different places in China.
7. The Gateway Arch was built as a memorial to Thomas Jefferson and the role Saint Louis played as the gateway to the West.
8. Answers will vary.

Page 117
1. A
2. D
3. B
4. C
5. C
6. B
7. pharaohs
8. renowned
9. mausoleum
10. symmetrical

Reference

Fountas, I.C. and G.S. Pinnell. 2001. *Guiding Readers and Writers: Grades 3–6*. Portsmouth, NH: Heinemann.